What people are sayi

I've known Fred Matser for many years. We collaborated on a major project to help children with leukemia. When we met recently in Moscow Fred told me about his many ongoing projects. He is a man with a big and open heart, and he is making the world better!
Mikhail Gorbachev, former Chairman of the Supreme Soviet and President of the Soviet Union.

Fred's recognition of cosmic consciousness as the driving force behind human life and society allows him to diagnose and offer healing solutions to our many challenges. This is an important book, whose message must be heeded.
Deepak Chopra, MD, best-selling author.

Fred Matser has led a fascinating life. He talks with passion on many subjects and shares his philosophy for our world and its future. May this book inspire others to follow his path.
Jane Goodall, PhD, DBE, Founder, Jane Goodall Institute and UN Messenger of Peace.

Fred Matser diagnoses our ills with x-ray vision and laser precision. He is able to extract himself from the cultural echo chamber of values, opinions and beliefs in which most of us find ourselves immersed, and then assess our situation from a neutral perspective. Fred renews and enriches subjects we thought we had already exhausted, by lucidly identifying and uncovering our blind spots. As it happens, these subjects are precisely those that are the closest to us, most integrally a part of our everyday lives. For this reason, the insights in this book have direct and very concrete bearing on how we think, feel and behave every day.

Bernardo Kastrup, PhD, philosopher and author.

Beyond Us

A humanitarian's perspective on our
values, beliefs and way of life

Beyond Us

A humanitarian's perspective on our
values, beliefs and way of life

Fred Matser

IFF
BOOKS

Winchester, UK
Washington, USA

JOHN HUNT PUBLISHING

First published by iff Books, 2020
iff Books is an imprint of John Hunt Publishing Ltd., No. 3 East Street, Alresford,
Hampshire SO24 9EE, UK
office@jhpbooks.com
www.johnhuntpublishing.com
www.iff-books.com

For distributor details and how to order please visit the 'Ordering' section on our website.

ISBN: 978 1 78904 551 2
978 1 78904 552 9 (ebook)
Library of Congress Control Number: 2020931273

A CIP catalogue record for this book is available from the British Library.

Design: Stuart Davies

UK: Printed and bound by CPI Group (UK) Ltd, Croydon, CR0 4YY
US: Printed and bound by Thomson-Shore, 7300 West Joy Road, Dexter, MI 48130

We operate a distinctive and ethical publishing philosophy in
all areas of our business, from our global network of authors to
production and worldwide distribution.

Contents

Acknowledgments

I am privileged to have had many teachers in my life, from those I know by name to anonymous people on the street whose behavior has inspired me in one way or another. And not only humans have been sources of inspiration: even animals and other expressions of nature have been great teachers.

My learning process now spans nearly three quarters of a century; too long a period for me to remember and mention all those who, directly or indirectly, have contributed to this work. So I shall restrict myself to mentioning my parents, Johan and Sophia, who were my teachers during my earliest days; my children, Nina, Saskia and Lyke; and my dear friend Bernardo, who has helped me tremendously at the present stage of my life, particularly with writing this book. To all these wonderful people, including the ones in between, whose names it is impossible to list here, I express my sincere gratitude for their helping me become who I am.

Above all, my deepest gratitude is to God, without whom we would not be here.

I hope this book offers you some support on your path. May it help you explore life with more trust in that which created — or, better yet, *continuously creates* — us in an ongoing process of forgiveness, so we can all find and experience unconditional love.

Preface

The privilege of introducing this work strikes me as both an honor and a difficult responsibility. How can I do justice to the refined, distilled results of a lifetime of piercing observation of the human condition? For this book embodies no less than that. The true extent of its value and impact will likely only be recognized by generations to come, aided as they will be by hindsight and perspective. For this reason, the responsibility that befalls me now is not only towards those who will read this volume during my own lifetime, but also—perhaps even *primarily*—the future.

I take on this responsibility only because I find myself in the privileged position of counting Fred Matser as a personal friend. Unlike great wise spirits of the past—such as Jung, Schopenhauer and Swedenborg—in whose company I can only bask in my imagination and dreams, Fred is a living presence in my life, not only an echo from times bygone. Over the past several years, I have had the opportunity to closely witness his ongoing meditations as they evolved and congealed. Without such fortunate perspective, I wouldn't dare do what I am about to attempt.

What better way to start, then, than to briefly introduce the man behind the message? It suffices to say this: Fred Matser's personality and life are the embodiment of what he says; he *is* his message come alive. Like the rest of us, he, too, started his adult life in the clutches of our culture's dysfunctional ways, his insights—his rediscovery of primordial truths—having evolved over time. But today his living example defines Fred and makes him unique, for I, regrettably, cannot say the same about many others; not even, frankly, about myself. 'Do as I say, not as I do,' the saying goes. But when it comes to Fred, if we all did as he does, the world would already be a very different and better place.

Not everybody will have the opportunity I've had to learn Fred's philosophy by sharing in a bit of his life and work. This is where the present book comes in: it makes his penetrating observations available to all, even those who will never know him in person. Goodness knows how badly we need it.

The defining characteristic of the essays in this volume is that they *pin down*, *magnify* and *mirror* back to us, with embarrassing clarity and force, our most dysfunctional yet unexamined ways of thinking, living and relating to each other in the early 21st century. Fred diagnoses our ills with x-ray vision and laser precision. He is able to extract himself from the cultural echo chamber of values, opinions and beliefs in which most of us find ourselves immersed, and then assess our situation from a neutral perspective. In doing so, he sees what most of us can't see. In the style of a true healer of the soul, he confronts us with unpleasant truths about ourselves, the acknowledgment of which is imperative if we are to heal and improve our lives. He points, too, to sane ways forward, whose appropriateness becomes self-evident once they are elucidated.

Each essay in this book—such as those titled 'Language,' 'Cooperation,' 'Money,' etc.—tackles a fairly broad subject. A reader's instinctive reaction upon reading their titles may be to wonder what more could possibly be said about such subjects, all already so well-known and discussed in depth. But here is where Fred's unique perspective shines: he tackles each subject from an angle hardly explored before, revealing important themes and considerations that somehow have gone largely unnoticed in our society. My own reaction to many of his ideas has been: "I had never thought of it this way…" I trust yours will be similar.

Fred can renew and enrich subjects we thought we had already exhausted, by lucidly identifying and uncovering our blind spots. And, as it happens, these subjects are precisely those that are closest to us, most integrally a part of our everyday lives. For this reason, the insights in this book have direct and very concrete bearing on how we think, feel and behave every day.

The power of Fred's observations rests on the fact that, once truly understood, they are *recognized*. It is this disarming recognition—this confrontation with our own collective shadow reflected on the mirror of Fred's lucidity—that makes this work so vital. It provides a sane reference point against which we can contrast the insanity of our culturally sanctioned choices. You won't find here any dead, linear, merely conceptual argument, but *living* reflections that penetrate far beyond the intellect. Fred touches us in places we've forgotten to defend or cover with our conceptual armor.

Although this is a book about the human condition—about our ways of being, behaving and interacting with one another—the observations in it are grounded in a metaphysics revealed to Fred through visionary experience, which he describes towards the end of the book. The core of this metaphysics is the idea that there is an *infinite*, transcendent reality that permeates, sustains and shapes (Fred would say 'in-forms') our everyday world of tables and chairs, as well as ourselves. This places Fred squarely in the mystical tradition called *Naturphilosophie*, whose luminaries include Albertus Magnus, Nikolaus von Kues, Paracelsus, Jacob Boehme, Robert Fludd, Johann Baptista van Helmont, Henry More and Emanuel Swedenborg. Many of them, like Fred, also received their knowledge through visionary experience; they have been to the same realm of infinite oneness that is the foundation of Fred's thought. We know it because they described what Paracelsus called the '*archeus*,' or '*vis formatrix*' or '*vis plastica*': a primal formative energy that, emanating from a transcendent infinity, pervades and shapes the finite world of matter. In Swedenborg's words:

all those who regard nature as the origin of all things to the exclusion of the infinite or who confuse the infinite with nature are but lesser minds and have scarcely reached the lowest threshold of true philosophy. For nature is only an effect of the infinite; the infinite is her cause. (As quoted by Ernst Benz in *Emanuel Swedenborg: Visionary savant in the age of reason*, 2002, Swedenborg Foundation, pages 125-126.)

If history is any guide, society isn't kind to those able to discern its ills through the mist of cultural apathy. A sobering example that looms large in my own intellectual horizon is that of Friedrich Nietzsche. Also a uniquely lucid observer of the contradictions of his time—to which his contemporaries were, by and large, thoroughly blind—Nietzsche was handed society's most demeaning verdict: complete and utter disregard during his sane lifetime. In the final weeks of his productive career, and with almost palpable pain, he confessed: "I live on my own self-made credit, and it is probably only a prejudice to suppose that I am alive at all." Driven to madness shortly after he wrote these words, his vision has ultimately proven uncannily prophetic. Some even suggest that the 20th century was born in Nietzsche's little rented room in a farmhouse in Sils-Maria, Switzerland, in the 1880's. Ignored at first, his thought eventually provided a much-needed map for a disillusioned and disoriented society emerging from the ashes of two world wars.

Unlike Nietzsche—who, in the words of Carl Jung, was like "a blank page whirling about in the winds of the spirit"—Fred is firmly *grounded*; grounded, in fact, much in the same manner that Jung himself was. It is no coincidence that their respective messages—Fred's and Jung's—have much in common. Fred's peculiarity—like Jung's—is that for him "the dividing walls are transparent." He is connected with a source—a 'place' in the soul where primordial truths still shine bright—that most of us have abandoned, lost from sight and no longer even remember. Whereas a few still manage to find their way back in rare moments of inspiration, being at the source is an effortless state for Fred. This confers urgent importance upon what he has to say. It is in that sacred, primordial ground—the *terra firma* of reality—that he makes his stand. It is from there that he tries to alert us to the thick and confusing fog of delusions and dysfunction that envelops our lives. It is from there that he shouts, "over here!" helping us to find our way back home.

His instrument is the book you now hold in your hands. May it open the doors to a different, better 21st century; may its message be heeded *faster* than those of its predecessors.

Bernardo Kastrup
Veldhoven, January 2020

Paths

It has become trite to say that ordinary human life has changed much since the time of our prehistoric ancestors. Nonetheless, I feel that most people today don't actually realize the sheer extent and repercussions of these changes, which have crept into our lives over the centuries. Back in our prehistory, our ancestors' inner lives were directly integrated with their outer, natural environment. There were no roads, sidewalks, street signs, or even demarcated trails, let alone GPS navigation. Every morning, as our ancestors awoke to go about their activities, a new *adventure*, a new *exploration*—quite literally—would begin through uncharted territory. They would have to sense and find their ways in their environment in a manner that has become unimaginable today.

Our ancestors had *freedom* in a sense lost to us. Now we follow roads, obey street signs and traffic rules, type in addresses in our phones. Every step we take, or kilometer we drive, is one already taken or driven countless other times by countless other humans. To say that we constrain ourselves to beaten paths doesn't begin to capture the restrictiveness of our situation, or its claustrophobic ethos. Our ways have become fully *standardized*, as opposed to spontaneous; driven by security and convenience, as opposed to curiosity and wonderment. Life has turned into a business, instead of an adventurous exploration.

Through the course of human history, going about the world has acquired a totally new meaning: now it has nothing anymore to do with *interacting*—in the true sense of the word—with our natural environment; we hardly sense it, negotiate with it, learn from it, or abide by it. We hardly even notice it. Going about the world today is merely a means to an end: it's about the destination, not the journey. If we could just teleport from one place to the other, so much the better. But since teleporters are still just science fiction, we've done the next best 'civilized' thing: we insulate ourselves from our natural environment. We use highways and roofed cars, as opposed to putting our feet on the ground, in the dirt or water, feeling the wind and the warmth of the sun on our skin, smelling the scent of wet earth after the rain.

Our early ancestors, unguided by streets or addresses, had to sense their way through virgin terrain, often never stepped on by another human. The world lay before them as countless possible paths, countless possible interactions, countless ways of seeing and being in the world. To know where they were and where to go next, our early ancestors looked at the position of the sun and other stars, sensed the direction of the wind, became acquainted with natural landmarks and vegetation, observed the behavior of other animals.

They were *attuned* to their environment through senses that have become atrophied in us, for sheer lack of use. For them, it wasn't all about the destination; it was about a *relationship* with the world where they were born, and which sustained their lives. Journeys for them were—instinctively—about new discoveries, new ways to relate, new experiences.

But now we no longer experience the richness of our ancestors' relationship with the world. In the name of safety, efficiency and convenience, we built—and continue to build—cages around ourselves; not only in the form of cars, houses and clothes, but also in the form of those ubiquitous *standardized paths*. Moreover—and perhaps most critically—this self-imposed confinement is both literal *and figurative*.

Indeed, as we *physically* confine ourselves to streets, highways and marked trails, we also *mentally* and *emotionally* confine ourselves to standardized ways of thinking and feeling. Human society offers us—in the form of culture—a menu of possibilities: liberalism, conservatism, materialism, spiritualism, communism, socialism, libertarianism and many other 'isms.' Each option entails a recipe—endorsed by the authority of labels and groups—for how to think and feel 'properly.' These are *mental roads*, so to speak, defined by words and to which we adhere as carefully as we adhere to the boundaries of a highway. They are tried, tested and therefore vouchsafed. God forbid we deviate from these standardized ways, for then we could lose the protection—and acceptance—of the group.

Without the reassurance we get from the echo chamber of group thinking, we might even question the validity of *our own* spontaneous feelings and intuitions. So we willingly forfeit our individuality—the unique and original way we have to spontaneously relate to the world, created by nature through billions of years of effort—for the sake of belonging, comfort and safety. As a result, the human adventure becomes more and more impoverished. Its bright original colors turn into bland pastels and, eventually, a mere greyscale. In some places and historical junctures, they have even turned into black and white. This is the tragedy of our situation.

Sometimes we can intuit the original richness and spaciousness of our ancestors' relationship with the world: have you ever noticed that, while hiking in nature, if you *return* from the hike along the same trail you used on the way over, you experience the trail in a completely different way? It's as though it were a different path. And this happens simply because you turned around to look back, instead of forward. Imagine in how many different ways we could experience a little piece of nature if we *left the trail* altogether, to explore it along different angles? Imagine in how many different ways we could experience life if we departed from the 'isms' altogether, and looked upon life according to our own spontaneous, idiosyncratic vantage points?

Alas, these days it is hardly possible to be 'off road' at whatever level or manner.

This is not to say that all paths are enriching. There are functional and dysfunctional paths, both literally and figuratively. Just as some trails lead us to the edge of an abyss, some ways of thinking are detrimental to life and world alike. But the point is that we lost our freedom to explore, to make *uncontrolled choices*. We've experienced some of this freedom when we were children. And largely thanks to the richness of that relatively unconstrained interaction with the world, which fed our souls in ways we cannot verbalize, our consciousness developed. But as adults, the opportunities for further development of consciousness become restricted by physical and mental roads and maps. We are *not* expected to find and experience original ways to think, feel and live. Instead, we are expected to *conform* to the standards available, including the reigning value-system of our culture.

By conforming we doubtlessly increase our safety and comfort. But we also become numb to our outer and inner natures and their unfathomable degrees of freedom. Instead of exploring the world we were born into, our lives turn into repetitive routines and formulas that fail to enrich us. Again and again we go around the same circle, to the point we become only half alive. We do live longer, but a kind of life more akin to surviving than thriving. Senses we originally had as children—a kind of subliminal intuition on the border of perception—

become atrophied. And without these senses, our ability to notice and pursue original, functional paths in life becomes diminished. We then find ourselves in a vicious cycle: by constraining ourselves to the standard paths, we lose the very intuitive senses that would allow us to pursue other, original, spontaneous paths. This, regrettably, is the reality we find ourselves in today.

So what can we do? How can we change? Simple things, surprisingly enough, may make all the difference. For instance, a simple daily meditation can help slow our minds, so we are *present* to the possibilities of the moment in our natural, peaceful state of being. Doing this daily can help wean us off our overwhelming addiction to the businesses and transactions of the anthropocentric world. Moreover, spending more time in nature contributes to wellness and wholeness as well. It re-grounds us in the matrix of our ancestral being, helping us recover lost perspectives.

Goals

The idea that the purpose and even the *meaning* of life is the achievement of certain goals—discrete events in time that we strive to realize—has become enshrined in our culture. Examples of such goals are reaching a certain pay grade, purchasing a certain type of car or house, or having a certain kind of partner. Today, a life without goals is often regarded as a wasted, haphazard, even irresponsible life.

If we attribute to a discrete event in time the whole meaning of our lives, we condemn ourselves to meaninglessness; for we either won't ever achieve the goal or—worse yet—*will* achieve it, at which point our life forfeits its meaning. What else are we to remain alive for, after that for which we've lived has become a thing of the past? To then focus on yet another goal just postpones the inevitable realization that no discrete event in time can ever embody a satisfying reason for living; they are all ephemeral like mayflies.

Such is the dilemma of modern humans. Our culture—as enforced by parents, teachers, supervisors, neighbors, friends, etc.—gives us a canned script to live by. According to this script, the meaning and purpose of life is the progressive achievement of a number of discrete, successive milestones: finish school, finish college, get a job, marry, buy a house, a car, have kids, get a promotion, then another promotion, retire, play golf... and? After one achieves a certain number of these milestones, one can't avoid a certain sense of having been cheated; for the meaning we derive from each of them seems to flash bright and intense like a lit match, just to burn quickly away. Once achieved, the realized goal recedes fast into the past, its meaning—at least after a few rounds of this game—evaporating. Perhaps more accurately, the goal's meaning reveals itself, once achieved, as the phantasm it had always been. All one is then left with is the final milestone conveniently ignored by the cultural script: death.

How many of us, in our deathbed, will have to confront the poignant realization that we've gone about life in all the wrong ways, focusing on all the wrong things? How many of us have regretted their choices and priorities only when it was already too late to do anything about it? How many have recognized the gaseous, insubstantial nature of goals only when—after a lifetime of dedication—they got close enough to run their fingers through the phantasm? Our canned recipe for living is based on smoke and mirrors; it remains persuasive only for as long as it is not seen with clarity.

When I see young, bright, ambitious people rushing to get that promotion, that sports car, that flashy house to impress others, I cannot help but be concerned about their future. What are they running towards? Dashing blindly straight to the abyss of meaninglessness—a phantasmal carrot hanging in front of their proverbial nose—they just don't know any better. Waiting for them on the other side of the abyss is the specter of death. Sadly, this is the lot of many of the brightest and cleverest amongst us: a mad rush towards... nothing. This is the script they inherited from our culture, for—despite the overwhelming disappointment of the majority—nobody seems to know what else to do instead. If not for our elusive, ephemeral goals, what are we to live for?

Yet, a meaningless life is entirely avoidable, provided that we look upon goals with discernment. Regarded as purposes in and of themselves, they are ephemeral and ultimately illusory. But when understood as useful elements in a broader context of meaning, their true role in the play of life becomes clear.

This is best illustrated with a metaphor: in the sport of sailing, sailors need to steer their boats in the direction of a succession of buoys, each of which they need to circle before adjusting course towards the next buoy. It would be ludicrous to regard reaching the buoys, in and of itself, as the *goal* of the sport of sailing; nobody sails for the sake of reaching buoys. Instead, people sail because something about the *process* of sailing is inherently fulfilling. The buoys are there just to *facilitate* the process by providing sailors with directions at each moment in time; they are merely helpers, markers, references in the sailors' relationship with the meaning of their sport, not the embodiment of that meaning. The placement of the buoys, while somewhat arbitrary, may enhance the fulfillment derived from the process of sailing if made correctly; for a challenging course brings out and intensifies whatever it is in sailing that sailors look for.

But just what is it that sailors look for in sailing? What is *meaningful* and *fulfilling* about it as a process? Why do people do it? These questions are hard to answer in a logical, utilitarian manner. Yet their answer is self-evident to those who sail. They do not need to tell themselves in words why they do it; they simply *feel* why. The meaning of sailing may be elusive to the intellect, but is very present, very real, very palpable to the sailor's intuitive feeling faculty.

Although we can't quite pin it down, we can try to talk *around* the meaning of sailing as a process. It entails a profound *communion* between sailors and the natural forces of their environment, a very intimate relationship. In contrast to automated yachts with engines, GPS navigation and what not, true sailors need to pull on ropes, point the sails in the right direction, feel the wind, sense the currents, watch the birds. As they negotiate the forward momentum of the wind and the resistance offered by water and its currents, sailors engage in a kind of tango with nature. They tune into the subtleties and nuances of the ocean and the atmosphere, their visible and invisible ebb and flow. They orient themselves by relating to the sun, moon and the stars of the night sky. True sailors *dance with nature*, therein residing the sensed meaning and appeal of their art.

Something ineffable about self and nature comes into focus as this dance unfolds; something that, once apprehended, reveals itself to be the very meaning of our presence on this planet. One seems to expand beyond personal boundaries, in a sense *becoming* nature itself, whilst preserving the perspective of a lucid observer. Both wordless insight and felt fulfillment seem to flow out from the depths of one's instinctive core, in a quiet but constant stream. This ineffable stream is the meaning of sailing, and it persists throughout the entire process. It doesn't vanish with the achievement of a goal—that is, with the circling of a buoy—but is inherent to every moment of sailing. Buoys merely provide directions to drive the process forward, ensuring its dynamism. While they aren't the purpose or meaning of the process, they keep it alive; for without the buoys—whether physical or imaginary, in the sense that sailors must always steer in the direction of *something*, some reference, some marker—sailing wouldn't even start. In a sense, they are an important 'excuse' for sailing.

Human life, I believe, is meant to be like sailing. Its meaning is immanent in each and every moment, not only in the ephemeral event of reaching and circling a buoy. Our goals are indeed important to provide us with impetus and direction, without which life wouldn't move forward. As markers indicating the course to be navigated, graduation, work, relationship, children, promotion, etc., are supposed to help us commune with our environment, interact with it, dance with it, thereby bringing to focus something ineffable yet crucially important about self and nature. However, we must not confuse references with purposes. Graduation, work, relationship, children, promotion, etc., in and of themselves, are *not* the meaning of life, in the same sense that reaching buoys, in and of itself, is not the purpose of sailing. The goals are not above the process; they are *instruments* of the process, subordinated to it.

Those who restrict the immanent purpose of life to discrete events—mere markers on the way—deprive themselves of meaning, in the same manner that a sailor who only enjoys circling buoys misses out on most of the fun of sailing. Since goals are intrinsically associated with a *time yet to come*, the actual, *present* life of these people—which is all any of us ever has—turns into an unfelt zombie march. By continuously reserving fulfillment for a future moment, they rob their present of its intrinsic meaning. Consequently, life turns in a mad and blind dash forward, for the present is never fulfilling, only the future might be. We must make haste, for there is no point in staying grounded in what is; all meaning is in what *might* or *must* be. And so forward we go, paying no attention to reality, missing out on the tango we are meant to dance with nature, so to ultimately arrive... nowhere. Through unexamined cultural conditioning, we cheat ourselves out of life.

On the other hand, those who realize that, although indispensable for powering and guiding our journey forward, our goals are mere buoys that define directions, meant to *facilitate* the realization of the meaning already inherent in each and every moment of life, keep their eyes on the ball and are aware of the context. They experience fulfillment and insight all the way into the gateway of death. Their lives are rich in significance, whether they reach and circle their buoys or not. After all, they are keenly aware that none of this is really about the buoys; the latter are just convenient references.

Your very reading of this essay has been a *process*—a *journey*—for you, esteemed reader, not only a goal in and of itself. Along the road that has brought you from the title to this closing paragraph, you've had a chance to dance with a world of ideas meant to evoke felt insights in your inner life. Culture will tell you that the sole point of this journey rests in how you can now *use* these insights so as to achieve some future goal. But is it really so? Is it how you *experienced* your journey? Surprisingly—and even frighteningly—on the answer to this question rests the realization of the meaning of life.

Competition

It is curious to see how beginners and casual hobbyists go about sports like tennis and table tennis: they don't really try to put the ball completely beyond the reach of the other player; instead, they seek precisely to *keep the ball in play* as long as possible. The longer the ball is in play, the more fun they have. There is even a popular paddleball game played on beaches—called '*matkot*' in Israel and '*frescobol*' in Brazil—whose object is precisely to *keep hitting* the ball for as long as the players can. When one of them fails to return the ball, there is an abrupt break in the flow of play that is experienced as anticlimactic. It is as though a dance were suddenly and annoyingly interrupted midway along the song. Don't get me wrong: each player does try to make the other work hard for returning the ball; but in doing so they are simply attempting to make the dance more challenging, stimulating, and the flow of play more engrossing.

In tennis and table tennis, however, at some point the object of the game oddly changes from keeping the ball in play to *defeating the opponent* and, thereby, interrupting the game altogether! The pleasure one feels becomes less immediate, less related to playing and more abstract, more related to a possible future win. The game changes from a spontaneous dance to a fight. Players even begin to invest their identity and self-image in victory and defeat: when they win, their self-image gets a boost; when they lose, they feel miserable about themselves.

This is a peculiar transition. Although we tend to take competition for granted in this day and age, the reason why competition has taken over most forms of organized human activity doesn't seem to be trivial. Some may claim that we are programmed by natural selection to compete, but the exact opposite can be argued: as pointed out by Yuval Harari in his book *Sapiens,* what got human beings to the position of dominant species on this planet has been precisely our ability to *cooperate on large scales.* Indeed, today we know that evolution favors cooperation just as much as it favors competition: ants, bees, termites and other social insects, not to mention innumerous relationships of symbiosis across species— such as that between clownfish and anemones— demonstrate it every day. Even our very bodies are constituted by communities of trillions of cooperating cells, many of which aren't even human.

It is distinctly possible, in my view, that our impetus to compete at all levels of life—from scoring higher than our classmates at school, to being promoted over our colleagues at work, to having the proverbial green*er* lawn that arouses neighborhood envy—is culture-bound. It is the value-system we inherit from our parents, teachers, bosses, friends and even strangers that induces our competitive behavior. This value-system tells us that, if we are to succeed, look good and have a good life, we have to do *better than others;* we have to be *winners,* not losers. It is a value-system that morally justifies *putting others down,* for this is the only way—allegedly—to secure our comfort and safety, as well as those of our loved ones.

If looked at closely, however, the underlying driving assumption behind culture-bound competition *is an illusion.* Competitors believe that, if they win, they will in some way feel better *than the* losers. But we can't—at any rate not ordinarily—access the inner life of another person to know how well or how bad she feels. We don't inhabit another person's body. We only ever know our own inner life; we only ever know how *we* feel, not others. As much as the outer behavior of a person defeated in competition—her gestures, expressions of frustration, etc.—may suggest disappointment or general displeasure, this shows only that the person feels worse than *she herself* would have felt if she had won instead. There is no objective, external reference point for determining if the winner feels better than the loser. All we ultimately have are our own inner feelings; everything else is merely theoretical abstraction, stories we tell ourselves.

Contrary to general belief, it isn't at all implausible that 'losers' may sometimes feel better than 'winners': a happy person living a harmonious life may be disappointed at being defeated in some competitive endeavor, yet still feel interiorly a lot better than a winner—although neither will ever know, as the comparison is impossible—who leads a generally somber and depressed existence. For the loser, losing may represent no more than a mild annoyance from which lessons can be learned, whereas winning may, for the winner, represent mere relief from the prospect of even more bitterness. We can only ever compare our feelings to *our own* feelings at some point in the past, under different circumstances, not to those of others.

Unassuming as it may sound, such observation completely undermines the very foundation of the scorched-earth competitive attitude inherent in our culture today: we believe that, by winning, we will somehow feel better than our competitors and, therefore, in an important sense, *be* better than they are. It is this illusion of being-better-than-another that motivates our competitive drive. But once we recognize the illusion for what it truly is, the whole mindset underlying our impetus to compete changes fundamentally: we no longer 'compete' as much as we play; and we play to better *ourselves*, not others. The dance of life becomes one of self-improvement and personal evolution, not a fight. The implications of this humble insight can not only be life-changing, but also planet-saving.

Unfortunately, today our whole culture runs on competition. Politicians have to win elections, business executives have to win accounts, students have to win scholarships, athletes have to win games; the list goes on and on. If we don't win from another, we aren't worthy. Even those who aren't playing feel the need to associate themselves with players so as to compete by proxy or projection: football supporters, for instance, by and large aren't invested in enjoying a beautiful game *per se*, but in seeing their team win. Media and advertisers alike prey on these projections—for instance, through the creation of heroic sports, business and political personas—in a parasitic relationship that distracts the population from the really important issues. Indeed, the whole of our economic system—which regulates all large-scale human activity—is driven by competition: we are rewarded for successfully taking as many resources away from others—and from the planet—as possible.

The problem with that attitude, of course, is that for every winner there has to be at least one loser; for every wealthy person there have to be hundreds, thousands, even millions in near poverty. And the planet isn't infinite, so eventually we will run out of resources to pillage. Moreover, our competitive way of life induces a kind of paranoia: surrounded by competitors on all sides—as we believe ourselves to be—we are constantly afraid that the person next door might steal our job, wealth, possessions, partner, etc. This fear, in turn, stimulates us to behave destructively and (preemptively) sabotage others. Perhaps even worse, a competitive system is an *exclusionary* one: if you have nothing to bring to the table that others might want to take from you, you are regarded as irrelevant. And so people in economically disadvantaged areas, such as parts of Sub-Saharan Africa, India and Bangladesh, are left to their own devices in the face of enormous challenges.

The need to win effectively *ensures* that most people end up disappointed and unhappy. In any corporation, for instance, a pyramidal management structure means that, for every ten or hundred employees vying for promotion to the next management level, only one will succeed and the rest will be left to lick their wounds in bitter disappointment. What a tragic, systematic waste of human drive! How much more could we accomplish in our society if we channeled our energies in more functional—or at least less dysfunctional—ways?

At a global scale, our competitive values motivate unbalanced accumulation of resources, money, indiscriminate pillaging of the planet and generally turn life into a paranoid nightmare dominated by fear. After all, to win one has to play, and in playing one risks losing. Even those who have already won still live under constant fear and stress, for their luck may turn and they may eventually lose the surplus that—through attachment—they have grown to consider indispensable.

Do we really need to live like this? Do we really need to make it so difficult for ourselves? I submit that we don't. It is true that tension and friction between participants in an economic system is beneficial—

perhaps even indispensable—to make the system more efficient, to stimulate creativity, motivate effective work and generally enable progress. However, for the same reason that *matkot* and *frescobol* players don't need to outright *defeat* their opponents so as to maintain the tension required for dynamic and rewarding gameplay, we don't need obsessive-compulsive, paranoid, scorched-earth competition so as to maintain the tension required for dynamic and rewarding economic activity.

Indeed, tension and friction are creative natural principles. They promote new ideas, new initiatives, new ways of being and living. They release latent energy and help shake off the old to make space for the new, so we don't get stuck in past failures or regrets. Even the act of lovemaking, from which life itself is created, metaphorically illustrates the formidable creative power released by tension and friction. While making love, what we experience is the tension of desire, the friction that produces—like two stones striking one another— the spark of something new, the intimate play of love in action; *not the wish to defeat our lover*. Lovemaking is the very embodiment of tension and friction as creative expressions of love.

Scorched-earth competition is just one of many ways to leverage these natural creative principles in a society, and a particularly *dysfunctional* one. A *functional* use of tension and friction would be one that, instead of optimizing for the *local* benefit of a few, contributes instead to the harmony and wellbeing of the *totality*. Today, however, our economic system is set up to seek local optima, to the detriment of the whole.

Why do we willingly sacrifice the wellbeing of the whole? It seems insane to do so, for ultimately everybody is worse off. We nonetheless do it because of the insidious, prevailing *assumption of scarcity*. We *believe* that there isn't enough to go around for everyone, so we need to compete to secure *our own* fair share. We are afraid of being left out. Instead of functional self-comparison—Am I better off today than I was yesterday?—we dysfunctionally compare ourselves *to others*—as if this were at all possible—to see if we are better off than they are.

Yet it isn't at all clear that there *really* isn't enough for everyone, provided that excesses and abuses are preempted. So instead of playing the dysfunctional game of 'comparing to win,' we could play the functional game of 'comparing with care so to share with care,' which optimizes for the whole-and-all. If we *all* carefully compare what we have in abundance with what others have in scantiness, resources can be redistributed so to minimize the number of 'losers' in the economic game at little cost to the 'winners.'

This is an attitude we could embody every day, in the most ordinary ways. Instead of checking to see if my neighbor has a better car than I do, or if my colleague got a promotion that I coveted—and then try to sabotage them to eventually get one-up on them—I could contrast what I have in excess against what others seem to lack. Instead of ranking others and myself according to how much we each have, I could rank others and myself according to how well we manage to balance out our resources for the overall benefit of us all. This is so simple and obvious as to sound trite. Yet, we don't do it, for this is not what society rewards us for.

To stimulate *functional* comparisons, it is imperative that our economic and cultural value-systems stop rewarding people for dysfunctional behavior. A never-ending local accumulation of profits and wealth, to the detriment of others, shouldn't be rewarded as it now is. Functional behavior, on the other hand, is often its own reward: as I know from personal experience, those who compare and share with care achieve an ineffable form of freedom and self-validation; they are no longer chained to the judgment of others; fear drops out and what moves them is love. We need a system driven by nurturing love and care, not fear.

This may all sound naïve and rather utopian, but the humble examples of *matkot* and *frescobol* illustrate how natural and innate this functional behavior is in all of us. We are born with it and it's all we have, until someone else tells us a different story that we end up buying into. We all have it in us to play the game just because the gameplay is challenging, beautiful and stimulating in its own right; defeating others just interrupts the game and ultimately makes life meaningless. After all, even those who only ever win eventually run out of adversaries and then ask themselves what they are alive for. We all have it in us to keep the ball going for the mere pleasure of keeping the ball going. We all have it in us to regard our fellow humans as valued members of our team, not as opposition. We *can* live a life without fear, paranoia, poverty and injustice. It is so simple to do so.

All we need is to see through the veil of insidious culture-bound values so as to remember the simple, primordial but profound pleasure of *just* playing. We don't need artificial, quantitative, abstract goals in order to enjoy the dance of life. When we go sailing, we don't do it for the mere sake of reaching a destination as fast as possible; we sail because we simply enjoy the *qualities* of the *process* of sailing. Analogously, we can play a productive, creative, challenging and functional economic game merely for the sake of playing it and improving ourselves, not for the abstract goal of winning a certain number of points. Beyond the level required for reasonable, comfortable living, financial goals are, in any case, like phantasms: once you get close enough to grab them, you realize there was nothing there to begin with.

It's okay to compare, provided that we do so for self-improvement and in order to share with care. It's okay to challenge each other, provided that we do so like tennis players who want to keep the ball on the court.

Community consciousness

Life is unquestionably nature's most complex manifestation. More than one scientist—amongst which Sir Robin Murray, one of the UK's leading psychiatrists— has referred to the brain as the most complex object in the universe. Indeed, the patterns of organization found in living organisms—from the molecular all the way to the intercellular level—are intricate to the point of exceeding our ability to fully comprehend. In non-biological nature, only crystals come anywhere near the simplest forms of life in terms of complexity. And beyond those, there is nothing even remotely comparable.

Next to complexity, there is one other key characteristic of life: the fact that—at least insofar as we are representative examples of what it is like to be alive—living organisms are *conscious*. That is, living beings have conscious inner life, feeling, experience. Somehow, the level of complexity of organisms seems to go hand in hand with the level of consciousness, as if the latter were the *organizing principle* underlying the intricacies of metabolism, the conductor directing the harmonious integration of myriad molecular and cellular interactions.

Our own body is made up of tens of trillions of individual cells, all of which cooperate with each other in fine-tuned lockstep to maintain life. Although our brain certainly plays a central role in ensuring this cooperation, we know now that much of the fine-tuning is achieved locally, in a decentralized fashion. Moreover, the brain itself is made up of about 100 billion neurons, so it too somehow coordinates itself in a decentralized manner. As we look into the details of the process of metabolism, we fail to find a centralized, discrete, measurable conductor anywhere. And yet the orchestra plays flawlessly most of the time, or we wouldn't be here. The complex, dynamic harmony of life seems to emerge out of nowhere — or, more accurately, *everywhere* — which suggests that consciousness itself, that immaterial quality of subjectivity so tightly associated with being alive, is somehow behind it.

The notion that consciousness organizes life has implications that contradict some of the key assumptions — or should I say, *prejudices* — of our current Western worldview. For starters, if consciousness organizes life, then it is more essential, more primary than life: it is consciousness that builds itself a material body, not a material body that somehow generates consciousness. Conflicting as it may be with present-day academic wisdom, from an experiential perspective the notion that consciousness is the conductor of metabolism feels quite natural and intuitive. As a matter of fact, our forefathers from ages past took it for granted that mind, psyche, soul, was the agency that built, maintained and repaired its body, not the other way around.

Moreover, if consciousness is the organizing agency of metabolism, it follows that it isn't localized or centralized, as Western science seems to assume. After all, the fine-tuning of metabolism is itself decentralized. Our body—the brain included—is de facto a *community* of cells with no central governing mechanism; its dynamically harmonious operation emerges out of *everywhere* in the space it occupies. Consciousness, therefore, must be a *non-local* organizing principle.

Ordinarily, we—humans—see ourselves as individual subjects confined to a certain region of space, largely isolated from other subjects and nature at large. We have this feeling of discrete 'me-ness,' of a *personal* identity, a disconnected self limited not only in space but also in time. "I am here and you are there," we think. Yet, our felt recognition of the intrinsic relationship between life and consciousness, plus the discoveries of modern cell biology, force us to reconsider this view.

You see, if life is a manifestation or expression of consciousness, then even single-celled organisms—which are certainly *alive*—have conscious inner life. The amoeba swimming in your toilet is conscious, and so are the trillions of *non-human* cells living in your gut—the so-called 'microbiome'—on whose proper functioning you depend for your own health. We aren't individuals to begin with, but *communities* of myriad *conscious* organisms, many of which aren't even human. We are each a team, a colony, a society, not an ego. The organizing effect of consciousness spreads its influence seamlessly across this entire society.

"But how can this be?" I hear you ask. After all, we seem to experience ourselves as *separate but unitary* individuals, not as colonies.

Clearly, then, *this experience of individuality must be an illusion.* If the organizing influence of consciousness is decentralized, spread seamlessly across space in a manner that doesn't recognize even the boundaries between species—think of your microbiome—then there is no such thing as truly *separate* conscious inner life. We aren't true individuals, and neither is the amoeba in your toilet or the non-human cells in your gut. We are all part of a fundamentally unitary whole, governed by non-local consciousness.

If a neuron inside your brain screamed, "Hey there! I am a separate individual here, alright!? I am my own man," you would laugh at it. If you cared to reply at all, you would tell your neuron that he is an integral part of you, not a separate little entity. Such a neuron would be merely neurotic, having forgotten its true role in the play of nature.

But when it comes to *us*, because we've lost touch with the higher perspective of life within which we are immersed, we don't recognize the delusion. Make no mistake, we are as deluded as that little neurotic neuron inside your head. But because *most* of us are deluded in *the same* manner, we reassure each other and take the delusion for normalcy. We don't see our craziness for lack of a critical mass of balancing counterexamples. We think our sense of 'me-ness' is quite alright, for its plausibility is backed by the cultural narrative we live under. It is as though most neurons in a brain suddenly started acting as separate individuals, instead of allowing themselves to be coordinated—that is, to be *thought* and to *be felt*—by the harmonious ebb and flow of the unitary field of consciousness within which they are immersed. They would all agree with one another that they are individuals, but something important would stop working one level up. After all, it's hard to imagine how a brain constituted by neurotic, egocentric neurons could produce a coherent thought.

The whole notion of individuality is a hallucination *of* consciousness, *in* consciousness; it is a faulty story consciousness tells itself. Neither we nor the cells in our body are true individuals, but instead integral parts of a unitary whole that far transcends us. All indications are that there is only one, non-local field of subjectivity that coordinates the complexity of life across the boundaries that seemingly separate organisms—and even species— from one another. There is only one living colony in nature, and that is the colony to which *all* living organisms belong. We are part of this one colony.

In a sense, our seemingly individual subjectivity is like a thought in a broader mind—which, in turn, has myriad other thoughts—just as the subjectivity of a neuron is like a little spark of experience within our own. Neither is truly separate or individual, but a segment of something bigger. When it comes to the neuron, we clearly understand this. But it has somehow become very difficult for us today to truly see ourselves as little 'neurons' in a bigger 'brain,' sparks of experience integral to a larger consciousness.

Living beings are *images*, representations of fully formed thoughts and fully formed feelings in universal consciousness. The Earth's ecosystems are like global metabolism, dynamic displays of planetary experience. The crystals that lay hidden in the bowels of the Earth, in turn, are seeds of thoughts and feelings *in the making*; pregnancies of manifestation. They link the organic with the inorganic, the living with the non-living. Yet, they too are *'in-formed'* —brought into form—by the universal organizing principle we call consciousness. The complexity of a crystal represents the early stages of 'in-formation' of a new planetary experience.

As a matter of fact, we shouldn't stop at crystals, for there are no natural boundaries to this line of reasoning. What we call life, metabolism, is just a particular *pattern of transformation* in nature, a recognizable dynamism that scientists identified and labeled. But beyond metabolism, nature is constantly transforming itself according to myriad other dynamisms. Just as the atoms, molecules and force fields in our body 'dance' together according to the choreography of life, the same sorts of atoms, molecules and force fields 'dance' together according to other choreographies we call 'storms,' 'volcanoes,' 'stars' and 'galaxies.' *Transformation* is the primary natural principle here, metabolism being just one particularly salient form of it. And if consciousness orchestrates the transformations underlying life, it must also orchestrate all other transformations in nature, the whole universal dance of existence.

Consciousness is the universal organizing principle that 'in-forms'—brings into form, shapes, orchestrates—the myriad dynamisms of nature, which manifest themselves as 'in-formed' transformation. The entire natural world is an *image* of universal conscious inner life, just as our own body is an image of our seemingly individual inner life.

The future of our civilization depends on our becoming cognizant of our true role in the whole-and-all. We are cells of a universal organism. Just like the cells in our body—which die and replace themselves constantly throughout the course of our lives, so as to maintain the integrity of our body—we too are temporary expressions of universal consciousness. Nothing needs to be mourned about our bodily death, just as we don't mourn the daily demise of millions of our skin cells. The birth and death of cells are integral to the movements and transformations of consciousness.

When cells in our body forget their role in the totality of the organism, becoming instead consumed by a deluded sense of *individuality*, cancer sets in. When the activity of cells ceases to the *'in-formed'* by the non-local field of consciousness that orchestrates the unfathomable complexity of life—thereby singing out of tune with the rest of the choir—tumors grow. Their mistaken sense of individuality leads to fear and a dysfunctional, ultimately parasitic attempt at self-preservation.

Some sense of individuality is useful and important, or we wouldn't know to which mouth to bring the fork in order to feed ourselves. But when this sense becomes an all-consuming delusion that breaks our inborn link with the universal field of instinct and intuition—the field of *transcendent* love—we become planetary cancers ourselves. We, and the planet, deserve a brighter future.

Cooperation

As I mentioned earlier, one of the defining characteristics of humans is our ability to cooperate with each other on large scales. Therefore, the subject of cooperation deserves its own treatment in this book. If nothing else, understanding how we succeed in large cooperative projects can provide valuable insight into how our minds work on a social level.

Big corporations are a representative example of large-scale human cooperation: tens of thousands of human beings work together towards largely the same goal, which is to build and sell a concrete product. Each person plays a small but important role in a structure much larger than any single participant. Each task fulfills a small but important function in a finely tuned mechanism. Each individual deliverable comes together with others to form a meta-deliverable, which itself comes together with others to form a meta-meta-deliverable, and so on, until the final product becomes a reality.

The coordination required for this is often mind-boggling and cannot be fully overseen by any individual person. The final product comes out of a manifold pipeline of great complexity, which starts with the extraction of raw materials—from water to rare-earth elements—and ends with a box ready for shipment to a customer. The number of individual steps that must seamlessly come together to result in a modern airplane, car, telephone or computer is extraordinary. Yet, our industry somehow manages it.

How can we get tens of thousands of human beings, working in many different countries, with different cultures, habits, laws, etc., to cooperate so precisely and harmoniously with one another, despite marked— often even conflicting—differences in their individual personalities, moods, preferences, personal goals, motivations and other idiosyncrasies? It seems almost miraculous, and yet we do it all the time. How is it possible?

The answer is simple: it is possible because they all have the same concrete, measurable goal. Those responsible for work coordination visualize the same end product and guide their teams based on a coherent overall context. If a large group of people knows what they are all trying to realize at the end, and if the result of their cooperation is measurable, they succeed in their joint enterprise. It is the *concrete mental image of the desired end result* that enables them to cooperate effectively, despite myriad personal differences; for that concrete image provides common references and context for communication and coordination. Different people can talk to each other and adjust their behavior on the basis of this common image or blueprint.

Allow me to elaborate a little more on this for—as you

shall soon see—it is an important point. Suppose you work at an automotive factory. Even though your work relates to only a small step in the entire manufacturing chain—say, you install the engine cylinders—in your mind you visualize the final product, the car. You know that those cylinders aren't merely being placed in arbitrary holes in an arbitrary piece of metal; you know the function they will perform and how they come together with other elements to form the car at the end. It is this *concrete mental image of the final product*—so concrete that you could even draw it in minute detail and show someone else—*and its function* that enable effective large-scale human cooperation. For if you realize that a cylinder isn't fitting snuggly into the engine block, as it should be, you know that this won't be a good thing for the operation of the car at the end. Hence you go talk to the person responsible for the engine block, so that the two of you can make appropriate adjustments. Again, it is the visualized image of the final product— its blueprint—that enables such communication and adjustment by providing a common reference, context and goal.

And this is the problem, for not everything that is important is amenable to concrete representation, precise specification and measurement. There are crucial things for our social health and wellbeing that can't be drawn on a piece of paper, or touched with our hands, or specified through a list of numbers. Indeed, there are a great many crucial things that can't be stuffed into a carton box. How are we to concretely visualize, say, community wellbeing? How are we to draw a blueprint of social harmony? How are we to quantitatively specify social cohesion? Can we *touch* personal growth? Can we *see* the development of our consciousness? Can we *hear* happiness?

It seems to me that, whereas we are well adapted to pursue external, concrete, measurable goals through large-scale cooperative projects, the same can't be said about the subjective world of our inner feelings. Yet, it is precisely our inner feelings that reflect the quality and meaning of our lives. What value is there in a great engineering feat if everybody is unhappy and depressed in the society that achieved the feat? External achievements are means to an end, and this end is how we feel inside; what else? If we can't coordinate our efforts at a social level to *directly* pursue our inner development, that which is of the greatest importance to us will remain elusive. This is our cruel dilemma. We haven't yet managed to emulate on the inside the successful collaborative strategies we've developed to tackle the outside.

The conclusion is as simple as it is alarming: either we strive to find ways to cooperate effectively in the pursuit of less concrete, less measurable, less palpable inner paths together, or we are each largely on his or her own when it comes to the most significant and defining purpose of our lives.

I, for one, know which of these two alternatives I prefer, and I even dare to suggest a way to go about it: if we were to give ourselves permission to be vulnerable in front of others, to expose our inner feelings at least to a trusted social circle, we could make steps in creating a shared context for communication and, consequently, cooperation. We could hold each other's hands and walk the inner walk together, in an atmosphere of understanding and support.

Although language—as we shall see later—is a flawed tool to communicate our inner state, we have alternatives: when we allow ourselves to be truly and unreservedly vulnerable before others, everything about our body—facial expressions, gestures, body posture, tone of voice, etc.—conspires to express how we truly feel. So we *can*—if we are willing to—engage in large-scale 'projects' of inner development; we don't need to walk that most arduous path alone, counting solely on our own individual strength. This is a journey we can undertake as a group, even as a society. We can help each other out, encourage each other, pull each other up when we fall.

The price to pay is merely to allow ourselves to be seen as vulnerable, which we all are anyway. It is a cruel illusion to imagine that, whereas we are weak, most other people are strong. As a matter of fact, the people who come across socially as most self-assured are often the ones most troubled within. Their self-assurance is just a defensive mask, a cloak, a compensatory maneuver they carry out subliminally, without even knowing it. At the end of the day, most of us are uncertain, confused, vulnerable and fearful most of the time, for we are all together in this strange and frightful condition of being living beings who know they will, one day, die. So why close, hide and defend our inner feelings, as if exposing them to the outside caused us deadly harm? For as long we persist with this attitude, we will remain alone in the most crucial challenge of life.

Things *can* be different. The choice is ours.

Knowledge

Little is more valued by us, 21st century human beings, than knowledge. We want—better yet, we *need*—to know what is going on, what the world is about, who or what we are. We need to know where we are going, *why* we are going there, the point of it all. Ignorance may be bliss, but the appeal of knowing is nonetheless irresistible.

Indeed, knowledge is that *felt* grasp or understanding of aspects of nature, including ourselves, which we tend to experience as reassuring and satisfying. It results from the integration, *in consciousness*, of information about self and nature at large. As such, we could say that knowledge consists in the *felt meaning* that arises when consciousness meets with information. Whereas there is a sense in which knowledge is shaped by information, there is an even more important sense in which information only becomes real—as opposed to mere abstraction—when it is transformed into knowledge by the touch of consciousness. Conscious living beings are the vessels wherein this alchemical transmutation takes place.

But *how* do we come to know things? By virtue of what faculties do we perform the transmutation and gain insight into nature and ourselves? Cognitive psychology tells us that we leverage a variety of cognitive functions to acquire knowledge, which can be roughly divided into two main classes: the *mental* and the *feeling* faculties. By 'mental' I don't mean mentation in general, but the intellectual aspects of mentation, our ability to *reason* towards knowledge through a chain of logical steps. By 'feeling,' on the other hand, I mean our ability to become *directly acquainted* with knowledge by somehow experiencing it in the body.

Although this is denied by the reductionist, materialist spirit of our time, it seems obvious to me — based on my own direct experiences — that both the mental and the feeling faculties allow us access to what could be described as *transcendent* information — that is, information that lies beyond our ability to perceive through our sense organs or derive through explicit steps of reasoning. Yet we can acquire the corresponding knowledge through *introspective intuition,* provided that we allow the influx of transcendent information — coming from *within* our inner world but *outside* our ego — to impress itself upon us.

The problem is that most people today are so busy *thinking* that the mental faculty becomes clogged — congested with self-generated reasoning under the control of egoic volition — and incapable of allowing transcendent, intuitive insights in. By the same token, most people are so overwhelmed with *emotions* that the feeling faculty becomes clogged — congested with compulsively self-generated personal dramas — and incapable of allowing transcendent, intuitive feelings in. It is as if God were trying to call us but the telephone line were always busy.

Indeed, we are so busy talking to ourselves, telling ourselves stories, chattering compulsively inside our heads and becoming afflicted by all this self-generated material, that we lose touch with the steady stream of transcendent information that would otherwise flow naturally into our cognition and inform our inner lives. Moreover, if and when we somehow let our guard down and allow the stream to momentarily impress itself upon us, we still don't take it seriously. Instead, we dismiss it and end up forgetting about it. We've closed ourselves up to transcendence and become consumed by our own personal, egoic subjectivity and its compulsive productions. Instead of participating in the natural flow of universal insight and feeling that surrounds us at all times, we've turned ourselves into isolated cognitive islands, too busy with themselves to even have an intuitive look around.

Our culture not only validates, but also stimulates this unfortunate state of affairs. Because most of us have clogged channels to transcendence, we've lost touch with it for so long that we've now concluded transcendence doesn't even exist. We then reinforce this conclusion in our social interactions to the point that it has turned into a *consensus gentium*. We all know that transcendence doesn't exist, don't we? While dismissing introspective, intuitive knowledge, our culture glorifies what we can learn through the mediation of the sense organs: the stuff we can see, hear, touch, taste and smell; the stuff we perceive *outside,* as opposed to whatwe can intuit *within.* The latter we've somehow come to consider suspicious, unreliable, merely subjective and 'psychological,' even though it constitutes the very essence of what it means to be a human being and, as such, the only carrier of reality we can ever know!

Science hypothesizes that our sense organs haven't evolved to pick out what is true—let alone *all* that is true—but instead to present the external environment to us in a way that facilitates our survival. We've evolved to perceive nature not in the way she truly is, but in a way that helps us survive. So what is actually suspicious is the so-called 'external' information conveyed by the five senses. Ultimately, we are subjective beings, our inner lives being the sole reality we ever become acquainted with. In dismissing our intuitive, introspective access to transcendent information and glorifying sense perception, our culture has conjured up a surreal and counterproductive epistemic inversion. We now call the illusion the truth and the truth the illusion.

And this is not all; the problem goes much deeper. Even if our mental and feeling faculties weren't clogged with compulsive thoughts and emotions, respectively, we would still suffer from the remarkable *imbalance* between these faculties under which we now live. By and large, we only truly trust our reasoning, our way to relate to the world according to steps of logic, be they deductive, inductive or inferential. If someone—anyone—is offering an opinion or a perspective on something, we expect this person to substantiate his or her views with an *argument*—that is, an intellectual story worded in language. Without it, we are liable to consider the person a loose thinker and their opinions baseless. If you can't *argue* your case, then you don't have a case—or so our culture sees it.

On the other hand, the streams of transcendent information that sometimes forcefully come through our feeling faculty, in the form of, for instance, artistic inspiration, are often considered operationally superfluous. Art is just for fun, enjoyment, it doesn't contain *actionable information* that could help steer our lives and our society; that could help change our views of self and world. Instead, art is seen as merely 'subjective' and not really true, a kind of aesthetic ghost devoid of substance. Artwork isn't regarded as a form of *communication*, as informative and significant as text or language (that is, the products of the mental faculty). At best, it is looked upon as an aside, an addendum, a mere nice-to-have. It conveys no substantial message—or so we tell ourselves.

The only phase of life in which the feeling faculty is still taken seriously in our culture today is kindergarten. There we pay attention to, and nurture, our ability to *feel* our way around. Children are encouraged to play, paint and generally express themselves artistically. Perhaps older people, too, are encouraged to produce art and explore their feelings in the last stages of life. But in between early childhood and late life, when adults are active and effectively shaping our civilization, this has been lost. The inevitable result is an equally unbalanced society.

Again, the reason behind such imbalance is that our culture thinks of the feeling faculty as something superfluous, not actionable, not truly informative. We don't take it seriously; we don't think we need it to determine the course of our society and inform our worldview. Instead, we only benefit from it in the form of innocent entertainment, to keep ourselves busy in a pleasant and harmless way. The feeling faculty has been effectively neutered, in that it no longer informs the choices and decisions that shape our collective future.

Yet, when allowed to, we often hold views and take actions based not only on steps of reasoning—intuitive as these steps may be—but also on *feelings*. Human beings are perfectly capable of feeling their way through life, if they but pay attention to their feeling faculty. Feeling is as informative as reasoning and should arguably be integral to decision-making at all social levels.

At this point, you may argue that feelings are unreliable; but so are logical arguments. How many a logical argument suffers from unexamined assumptions, circular reasoning, false premises, conflation and a host of other logical fallacies that escape our attention? Moreover, we cannot logically defend the validity of logic itself without arguing circularly, which shows that logic is, in some sense, arbitrary; it is largely a kind of best-practice, a heuristic tool that works but which we have no reason to regard as fundamentally or ultimately true.

The bottom-line is that both our key cognitive faculties—the mental faculty and the feeling faculty— can provide access to valid information in different ways; they can both be *informative* and are both important capabilities mother nature has endowed us with. At the same time, they can also both be unreliable, depending on circumstances. Sorting wheat from chaff is the individual challenge each of us faces when trying to cognize nature and ourselves, irrespective of which faculty we use. But disregarding one faculty for the sole benefit of the other, as a matter of principle, is an artificial and rather brutal amputation of a cognitive organ. We don't need to do it, have nothing to gain by doing it and, in fact, much to lose.

We must re-learn how to feel—and then trust our feelings—just as we know how to think and trust our thoughts. Feeling, if unclogged by emotion, is almost like a sensory organ that unveils important things about nature and the universal order of things. Yet, unlike the five sense organs, true feeling is achieved through introspection. Contradictory as this may sound to the intellect, reconciling these characteristics of the feeling faculty is key if we are to, once again, live in whole and harmonious balance.

Indeed, if we are to regain access to the streams of transpersonal, transcendent information that surround us at all times—but which we've become blind to—we must unclog both our mental and feeling faculties. Instead of imposing the will of our ego in controlling and directing what we think and feel, we must *allow ourselves to be thought, allow ourselves to be felt.* This entails a kind of letting go of our own opinions, traumas, beliefs, emotions and preferences; an attitude of receptiveness and absence of judgment that allows the deeper levels of our consciousness to take initiative and inform us of what, from *their* perspective, we need to know. The corresponding state of consciousness could be described as an open, deeply meditative state, wherein the brain operates in the slower rhythms science refers to as 'delta waves.'

This much-needed unclogging must happen in equal measure for *both* the mental and feeling faculties, so neither dominates the other but, instead, *cross-fertilize each other in a synergistic manner.* This is the only way for us to develop a balanced picture of ourselves and the reality we inhabit, instead of clinging to partial and distorted views, aberrations our social consensus has come to take for the truth.

Art

I never cease to be astonished by good music, always wondering how it is possible for a mere human mind to come up with such melodies, such rhythms and arrangements. Some pieces of music—I now have Noa's "Ave Maria" in mind—seem to defy their own simplicity, as if a divine presence stood behind the notes and came into our world through them. Often, I just can't believe that our minds can create such extraordinary compositions.

And perhaps indeed they don't. The most remarkable works of art—whether music or painting or any other art form—seem to be *downloaded* from somewhere, not created. They seem to come into our world *through* a human mind, but not *from* it. The artist's talent has to do with their ability to functionally connect with a transpersonal sphere of primordial creativity. Once connected, the artist simply 'hears' or 'sees'—with his *inner* eyes and ears, not merely his sense organs—a primal, archetypal template, which he then notes down. As such, the artist is a conduit to a transcendent realm.

Over the course of history, we have invented means for allowing our artists to *capture* and then *share* their unique inner experiences with the rest of us. Taking music again as an example, we have invented a code— musical notation—which allows the artist to record what he has experienced while it is still fresh in his mind. And then we have come up with musical instruments to *reproduce* the inner experience the artist originally had, so it can be shared with the rest of us. If you think about it, this is an extraordinary human achievement: it has allowed all of us to share in an experience only a few of us have firsthand. Our artists are explorers that go out into a transpersonal realm of primordial creativity and return with gifts for the rest of us.

More than just recording the inner experience they had, artists also *elaborate* on it afterwards. This elaboration of the material received is important, for it is what makes a work of art *alive* in our world. What is downloaded is often but a *seed*, which needs to be nurtured, cared for with tender love, so it grows, develops, unfolds its intrinsic potentials under the guidance of the artist. It acquires a life of its own by being *interpreted* in myriad different ways. Sometimes the interpretation is done by conductors: the same piece of music can sound different in subtle, nuanced ways in the hands of different conductors. Other times the interpretation is done by composers themselves: take, for instance, the European musical theme called Folia; for hundreds of years it has been continuously reinterpreted in the most wonderful ways by different composers, showing no signs of being exhausted. Folia is a seed that came into our world *through* an original artist, who noted it down and gave it a life of its own by releasing it into our world. And it is still alive and unfolding today.

The job of an artist is thus to give *expression* to primordial templates in the mind of God, which have existed since the beginning of time, just waiting to be tapped. Through the artist, God's creativity comes alive in our world. And unlike our own human mind, the divine templates—original 'modes of vibration' of God's creative impulse that imprint themselves on the mind of an artist—have no *opinion*. Instead, they just *are*, as spontaneous vibrations of a divine instrument. In a world divided by opinions as ours is—just think of politics, for starters—the influx of divine creativity enabled by artists is like a healing balm. We need it to treat our self-inflicted wounds, for it is through art that our polarized, dysfunctional world is brought together again with its divine source.

Artists aren't superfluous. Art isn't merely a 'nice-to-have.' Instead, it may very well be what is holding our precarious world together. Art is a revitalizing link back to our source, which keeps us sane insofar as it is at all possible to remain sane in this largely dysfunctional society. Without art we would be uprooted and adrift, disconnected from the very ground of our being, separated from God. Art is the remaining umbilical cord our life and sanity depend on, now that even true religion—by which I don't mean fanatical dogmatism— seems to be falling by the wayside. We need art and the artists who coax it—like midwives—into our world.

Self-expression

There was once a little girl called Mary, who lived in a big country house with her parents. She had a whole bedroom only for herself, with a large window through which—with the help of a little wooden bench to climb up—she could see the canopy of a great big oak tree in the backyard. She often peeked into the secret lives of the birds and insects inhabiting the tree, which provided endless entertainment for her curious mind.

By the time autumn set in, however, the world outside had turned grey and uninteresting. The birds, insects and colored leaves were gone, and everything looked damp, bare and dead. Even the chic wallpaper of Mary's bedroom—which her mother had just replaced with much effort and care—was grey and plain like the sky outside. Mary had once overheard her mother say to her father that the wallpaper was 'elegant' and 'of good taste,' but none of that meant anything to her.

Then, on a rainy morning, upon noticing her large box of colored crayons lying on the floor of her bedroom, Mary had a sudden inspiration. In contrast to the wallpaper and the weather outside, the vibrant colors of those crayons evoked life, excitement and joy. It was a Sunday, there was no school, and Mary's parents were busy reading the newspapers downstairs.

Seeing in the plain wallpaper an invitation for creative

expression, Mary wasted no time. The wall was like a canvas open to her imagination, waiting to be filled in. She could hardly contain herself, so at once she began bringing life into it with the colors, forms and characters that gave expression to her inner world. Spontaneously and with increasing excitement, the images poured out onto the wallpaper, mirroring the life Mary felt within herself. After a short while, an entire world of fun and beauty inhabited her transformed bedroom wall. Mary felt alive, in flow, expressing herself as nature meant for her to do. That rainy, grey Sunday morning was transmuted through the magic of her creative expression. What a wonderful morning, what a wonderful world, what a wonderful life.

And then Mary heard steps on the staircase: her mother was coming up. Mary froze, suddenly awakening from her spontaneous artistic 'dream.' She had completely forgotten about her mom. Her bedroom door opened and there she was, her mom, three times taller than her: "What have you done?! We've given you new wallpaper and now you've ruined it! You're not getting your candy today and we'll cancel Charlotte's visit for this afternoon! That's your punishment."

By now Mary was cowering in a corner of her room as the gigantic—and awfully menacing—frame of her mother stood over her, crushing her into submission and near panic. Mary couldn't understand what was going on. Her mother, who had always been a source of love and safety, was now a terrifying presence. What had Mary done wrong? Was it so bad to express her creativity? Weren't the drawings beautiful?

Apparently not. Judging by her mother's violent reaction, she had done a terrible thing. But why? Mary had drawn with crayons on sheets of paper before and her mother always told her, very gently and serenely, how nice it all was. What was different now? Mary couldn't wrap her little head around the seeming arbitrariness—even madness—of the situation.

Marked by this seminal event in her childhood, Mary figured that the only safe thing to do was to keep her inner life hidden very deep inside. You never know how people will react if you openly express yourself. They may turn into mean monsters; even one's own parents, who are supposed to be protective and supportive. So Mary closed herself up like a clam. It was best to just learn and follow the rules and conform. The message conveyed by her mother's reaction was crystal-clear: the world is a threatening place. It doesn't give a damn about what you think, feel or want. People don't want to know what you have inside you; they even get pissed off and might hurt you if you show it to them. All they want is that you follow the rules. Mary learned, alright. And conformed. She became a good student and later a successful professional. But she never again dared to express her feelings and emotions spontaneously, despite having tons of them.

We live in a world of Mary's. Our lives are only partial, often even precarious, for it is too important to make sure most of our inner world remains hidden inside. It's the only way to feel somewhat safe. Therefore, in an important sense, we are only half born. A huge and important part of ourselves—often *the* most important part—never sees the light of day. We participate, at best, only half-heartedly in what was supposed to be the dance of human society, but now looks more like a march of frightened drones. Too insecure are we, to open up. Adults have taught us that this is a game of conformance, not of spontaneous self-expression.

And we are all so much the worse for it. You see, children aren't empty, malleable vessels to be taught rules so as to act mechanically. They don't come to us simply to conform to the peculiar and ephemeral—often even arbitrary—value system of this particular culture, at this particular point in history. No, a child has a rich, living, vibrant, unique inner world. Each child is a gift to society, for each carries an original contribution to *our* world: a talent, a way of seeing things, a vision, a potential for expression. The child we see is like a gift-wrapped box, hiding riches inside. But if the box never opens, the gift is wasted. The way we relate to our children today ensures that the box never fully opens.

We, as parents, educators and guardians, have the responsibility to help our children engage fully with our world and contribute their gifts to our society. But first, *it is we who have to go into their unique inner world, engage them on their level, in their own language,* so they turn into self-confident, open adults. Only then can they meaningfully contribute to *our* world. Only by being able to relate to us in a safe, stimulating, nurturing way, can the new entrants of our society express their true, unique selves to the full, so to enrich the lives of us all.

We receive over a hundred million brand new gifts each year on this planet. Each unique, each a precious gem. Once, we were such gifts ourselves. Yet, instead of allowing them to add their unique color and style to the 'van Gogh' of human society, we force them to comply with a black-and-white set of procedures designed to make our neurotic selves feel just comfortable enough to avoid the nuthouse. We impose our insecurities and fixations on them, thereby washing out their colors.

Luckily, we have guiding examples that show us a better path forward. I have a good friend called Jane, who once told me a wonderful story of her childhood. Each morning, her mother would come back from the chicken pen with eggs to fry for breakfast. Little Jane wondered where those eggs came from: her mother would collect them in the morning and, by some kind of magic, *new* ones would pop up in the chicken pen the next day. This was a great mystery that needed elucidating. So one morning little Jane woke up in the wee hours, even before the chickens. Stealthily, she dressed up, opened the backdoor and went into the yard. Once there, she carefully opened the chicken pen and sat inside, next to the chickens, patiently observing. Hours passed until she realized, when one of the chickens stood up, that the eggs *somehow* came from under the chicken! This discovery—the fulfillment of curiosity—was one of Jane's seminal childhood moments.

In the meantime, Jane's mother had woken up and was frantically looking for her. She was very concerned about her daughter, until she noticed a little kid squatting amongst the chickens in the backyard. Despite being very nervous by this time, Jane's mother walked calmly towards her daughter and squatted down, so as to be at the same level as Jane. She then proceeded to say something to the effect of: "Oh, you came to fetch some eggs, didn't you? How nice of you. But, Jane, let me share something with you: I was very worried because I didn't know where you were. So, next time, could you tell me where you are going?" Jane understood her mother and immediately agreed to the request.

Because Jane's mother was wise enough to come down into *Jane's* world, Jane's curious and investigative nature blossomed. She went on to become an amazing scientist and, today, we have *Jane Goodall*, the primatologist whose scientific work has enriched our society and lives with hues never before seen. Like her mother, Jane has been able—with exquisite sensitivity—to enter the inner world of other living beings—chimpanzees and other primates—and relate to them in their language, so to bring to our society perspectives never before dreamed of.

Imagine what a society of Jane's, instead of one of Mary's, could mean for our lives.

Language

Language is such a magical tool. It allows us to construct alternative realities purely with words, stories about characters and events that never were, except in our imagination. Moreover, language gives us the magical chance to plant, in the mind of another human being, thoughts and images born in our own. Indeed, this is precisely what I am doing right now: sharing with you, through these words, intimate aspects of my inner life. Without language we arguably wouldn't be really human, for structured verbal communication is—at least to a large extent—that which defines our humanity amongst animals.

Yet, there is a dark side to this magic, one that most of us—unfortunately—aren't aware of. To see it, notice first that the birth of language was motivated by the very simple, *practical* need to have essential information communicated amongst our ancestors. For instance, they needed to tell each other where food was to be found, to warn each other of lurking predators, and to coordinate their activities during a hunt. As such, language originally evolved to refer to *objective* things and events in the *outside* world: places, creatures, activities. Perhaps only much later did we try—largely unsuccessfully—to augment this survival tool to convey some of our *inner* world.

Consequently, language is much more conducive to practical descriptions of the world outside than it is to capturing the subtleties of our inner lives. We can describe objective things and events accurately and with little ambiguity; but when it comes to planting into the mind of another the complex gestalt of our inner feelings and intuitions, language is often a rather cumbersome and limiting tool.

In and of itself, this doesn't need to be an issue. However, *we tend to forget that language is limited.* We don't remind ourselves of its innate boundaries. Instead, we take for granted that everything of significance can be completely and appropriately captured in words. Yet much of it can't; much of it is too subtle, too delicate to survive the rough and blunt touch of language; much of our inner lives escape the grip of words like sand slipping through clenched fingers.

Therefore, because human society and culture are based entirely on language—the only available tool for bridging the gap between minds and erecting the *collective* structures upon which a civilization is built— society and culture are blind, as a result of such linguistic reliance, to much of our inner lives. People are valued almost exclusively on account of what they articulate in words. If a person's inner spirit harbors rich gems that they just can't express through language, the person will nonetheless often be regarded poorly. Moreover, whatever a person *does* say, we tend to assume that it accurately represents what the person *means*. Yet our verbal utterances often don't express the essence of what we experience from the inside, either because we aren't eloquent enough or because we—inadvertently— use our words for manipulating others. Language— including the tone and rhythm with which it is verbally articulated—can often be a dysfunctional representation of our inner state.

Nonetheless, we often judge people based on what they say, not what they might be *trying* to say. We have little patience to invest extra effort in avoiding misunderstandings. We also pretend—without even realizing it—that whatever can't be said doesn't actually exist. How absurd! How much misjudgment have we passed on our fellow humans? How much injustice have we committed towards others, and even ourselves, on account of linguistic limitations?

Remarkably, we instinctively know to adopt an entirely different attitude when it comes to babies and toddlers: we don't judge them for what they *can't* express, or the clumsiness of the sounds, gestures, facial expressions, etc., through which they try to communicate. We know there is much more to their inner lives than what they can *say*. We do our best to communicate with babies and toddlers in ways beyond words, couched in an attitude of forgiveness and tolerance. Why do we lose this attitude towards adults?

Perhaps because we've come to a point where only the

naked vulnerability of a baby or toddler can effectively disarm us; can put us in touch with an intuitive understanding ordinarily repressed by our culture; can remind us of the rich inner realities—complex, nuanced gestalts of thoughts, feelings, images and intuitions— hidden behind the opaque curtain of language; can inspire us to protect and nurture that which can't be directly communicated, for we intuitively sense its importance.

When it comes to adults, however, the patience, tolerance and sensitive attention we reserve for babies seem to evaporate. Because grown people—unlike babies and toddlers—hide their vulnerability behind an armor of social posturing, we assume that adults are somehow immune to the challenges and limitations of linguistic expression. We act as though everybody could transparently and clearly convey the full richness of their inner lives through words. Therefore, we judge them based on what they manage to *say*—or *fail* to say— as opposed to what they mean or how they actually feel from inside.

Language—appallingly—has made empathy seem redundant. We no longer strive to put ourselves in the shoes of another; instead, we judge the other's utterances. The latter is much easier and more convenient, so we are covertly motivated to take it for a fitting substitute.

Yet we know, from *first-person experience*, how difficult it is to properly express ourselves. We know that much of the vulnerability of the toddler we once were survives intact in our adult selves. We just—for some strange reason—don't apply this first-person understanding to others, even though they are humans like us. We don't extrapolate what we know about ourselves to others of our own kind.

And as if this weren't bad enough, when people bravely *attempt* to express their feelings in words, often they aren't taken seriously. Because language, by origin, is so strongly grounded in *objective* references, the linguistic expression of something eminently *subjective*— such as our inner feelings—can sound awkward and make a person look silly. This misperception is then enshrined in an implicit cultural value-system that associates the utterance of feelings with—of all things— *weakness*. As a result, many of us put on a mask of callous objectivity, which only reinforces the skewed, unnatural value-system that motivated our defensive posturing in the first place. It is a linguistic vicious cycle that—absurdly—relegates the naked reality of a human being's inner world to the fringes of our way of life.

Despite their dysfunctional limitations, words have gone past merely mediating communication: now we even *think* in language. We internalized words to a degree probably unimaginable to our early ancestors. Beyond talking to others through words, we now talk *to ourselves* in words. Our inner lives have become dominated by inner *chatter*, instead of the rich, spontaneous imagery and intuitive cognition that probably suffused the spirit of our ancestors. Worse yet, even our emotions have become enslaved by words: it is the semantic content of our inner chatter that triggers our passions. We *talk* ourselves into sadness, angst and despair. In the meantime, the *real* reality passes us by.

Indeed, because all we ultimately have are mental representations, we've managed to replace the actual world with a story, an internal narrative. Our lives now effectively consist of what we *tell ourselves* is going on, instead of what is *actually* going on. Even our sense of identity is determined by a narrative; one so powerful we fail to distinguish our true selves from it. *We've effectively replaced reality with stories.* What is really going on has been hidden behind the opaque curtain of words.

This is tragically dysfunctional, for words were never meant to capture and reflect the whole of reality; they just *can't* do that. Language evolved merely as a practical tool for simple, practical purposes. By hiding reality behind a narrative—a culture-bound story we internalize—we blind ourselves to a great many things of tremendous significance and import; things that can't be *said*, so I won't even try to say them here. One can only become acquainted with them through direct experience, unmediated by language.

Words can insulate us from the ineffable lushness of direct experience. What we feel when hearing a description isn't nearly as rich as the firsthand experience, 'in the moment,' of the thing described. Moreover, because it takes time for our minds to translate direct experience into words, the story we tell ourselves about what is going on always refers to a *past* state of affairs. In other words, descriptions are a form of documentation of the past. Language not only insulates us from the richness of the true world, it also separates us from the *present moment*, which is all there ultimately is. By the time we translate a direct experience into the words of our internal chatter, the experience itself has already passed us by. Sadly, all we then remember is the story we told ourselves *about* it, not the experience itself. We exile ourselves from the here-and-now without even realizing it. While naively believing to be open to the world, we are in fact sealed inside a cocoon of internal narratives.

Our present condition is so unnatural that there must be some irresistible, covert psychological gain behind it. And indeed, there is one so compelling that it may singlehandedly explain the whole of our dysfunctional love affair with words: *language allows us to repress and dismiss our passions under a blanket of syntactical rationalizations.* Instead of having to confront the demons within us—our deepest fears, traumas, regrets, frustrations, impossible longings and unrealizable dreams—we cleverly *explain them away* through articulate linguistic constructs. We tell ourselves stories that justify our appalling lack of care and attention for the depth and aliveness of our inner world. Instead of facing, embracing and ultimately integrating our demons—turning their formidable energy into a *functional* force—we alienate and render them dysfunctional. As a result, lost and unchecked in the forgotten depths of our soul, the demons usurp ever more energy and eventually erupt in unexpected and uncontrollable ways. Language, in the form of our inner chatter, has helped us turn our own souls into enemies, into veritable time bombs. Language has enabled us to rationalize the difficult facets of our inner lives away in a culturally endorsed game of make-believe.

Things don't need to be like this. We have the keys to the prison's doors, for we created the prison—our anthropocentric world—ourselves, with the bricks and mortar of words. The prison only exists insofar as we *tell ourselves* that it exists. It has no independent reality, no power of its own. The *real* world is alive and pulsating under the thin cover of narratives that separates us from it. It wants to be rediscovered, for this is nature's way. We are born with the capacity to relate *directly* to it. We have always had the sense organs and the intuitive cognition needed to embrace it once again. To rediscover the ineffable riches surrounding us requires no effort, no action, no doing; much to the contrary: all we need is to *let go* of the incessant chatter in our minds, so to *allow* ourselves to be guided by reality.

Growth

In this day and age, the word 'growth' has come to play a key role in almost everything we consider important and desirable. Everything now is about 'growth': economists talk of economic growth; business leaders talk of revenue and headcount growth; politicians of employment growth; geographers and statisticians of population growth; speculators of share price growth; etc. And 'growth,' of course, is directly related to another key word in our society: 'bigger.' We want bigger cars, bigger houses, bigger televisions, etc. Everything must get bigger. Now, since 'growth' is what leads to 'bigger'—or so we assume—we've come to associate prosperity and wealth with it.

But where does this little word, 'growth,' come from? Before there were structured economies, a job market, elected politicians, or even money, there was already growth. What did it mean back then? What kind of phenomenon did we describe with that word? The answer is pretty straightforward: originally, the word 'growth' was meant to describe *organic, natural growth.*

Our ancestors lived in a world where *natural* growth surrounded them. They could see new shoots and flowers growing from trees every spring. The ones who lived longer could even notice that the trees themselves grow. They saw people grow from newborn babies to fully formed adults. They saw grasses and weeds miraculously grow from seemingly dead soil after the winter. What they understood as growth was *a function of nature*, a primordial principle, not a human construct such as revenue growth; it was a phase in the natural cycle that governed their lives, and which also included birth, flowering, decay and death. In a sense, growth for them was a thing of the gods, the visible image of a transcendent process beyond their understanding. Growth was... well, *magic*.

Our society has hijacked and distorted the word 'growth.' It has now become an abstract concept related to numerical *quantity*, not natural *quality*. Growth is represented as a line on a graph—usually pointing up—displayed on a computer screen. What could be more distant from our primal understanding of growth as evolving *qualities*, the concretization of inner potentials, the awakening of sleeping powers, the release of intrinsic vitality?

To merely make something bigger doesn't imply growth in its authentic, original and natural sense. A bigger society—in terms of population, gross domestic product, territory, or any other quantifiable concept—is not necessarily a society that has *grown* in the authentic sense of the word. How about the growth of empathy? How about the growth of harmony or wellbeing? How about the growth of consciousness? *Authentic growth is a qualitative unfolding of latent inner potentials*, not the multiplication of units; it's about becoming who we really are, expressing our dormant powers. Unlike economic growth, authentic growth is always functional. This is what nature has taught us, but we misunderstood and misused her lesson.

What we now call 'growth,' contrary to authentic growth, is dysfunctional. Economies and populations cannot keep on growing forever, for the planet itself is getting no bigger or richer in resources; it can't accommodate continuous 'growth.' Therefore, if we link our wealth and wellbeing to economic growth, we are bound to face a dystopian future—if any future at all. The association we've made between wealth and economic growth, prosperity and quantifiable parameters, does not serve us well. True wealth and prosperity arise from *authentic, natural* growth, the *qualitative* development of our consciousness, the organic unfolding of our inner potentials.

You see, it is true that growth is to be desired; it is true that the purpose and meaning of our lives on this planet is intimately related to growth, *authentic* growth. But we have sabotaged ourselves by twisting the meaning of the word. Now, instead of seeking our authentic personal and social growth, we chase abstract numbers. We project the numinous, transcendent glow of authentic growth onto quantities and pretend that this projection is real. And so we end up chasing numbers, not authentic growth. We chase phantasms conjured up by our own deluded minds. And since we can never really catch a phantasm, we never really get to where we hope to get. The numbers are never high enough. We never experience satisfaction, and so keep on working tirelessly to make the numbers ever bigger, till one day we will either wake up or destroy the planet and ourselves along with it.

Hidden costs

Life has a cost. As living beings, we must consume resources in order to maintain our structural and dynamical integrity—that is, to survive. We must consume oxygen from the air we breathe, as well as calories, proteins, vitamins and minerals from the food we eat. We must consume energy to keep ourselves warm in the winter and cool in the summer. We must consume water to maintain the flow of our metabolism. And then we choose to consume a whole lot of resources of nearly every kind to move around in automobiles, do our work conveniently and entertain ourselves. All these patterns of consumption entail costs in some form, for not only are the resources we consume *taken* from somewhere, the waste we produce as a result must also *go* somewhere. Someone or something somewhere is paying for it.

However, our society has invented unbelievably clever and subtle ways to hide the true costs of our way of life, so as to encourage ever more extreme patterns of consumption and sustain the holy grail we call 'economic growth.' This camouflaging of true costs is largely deliberate and happens at multiple levels.

The first and most obvious level is that we hide from ourselves, as effectively as possible, the pollution we generate. What if we built our industrial zones bang in the middle of residential areas, instead of hiding them away in less populated peripheries? What if we dumped our waste in landfills adjacent to where we live? What if the insufferable business of dismantling decommissioned seagoing ships—which is now tucked safely away on the shores of India and Bangladesh—took place on the beaches we frequent? We would be reminded, daily, of the foul-smelling fumes, the harmful noise and destructive waste we constantly excrete into the environment. Very quickly we would begin to ask ourselves whether this is the society we want to live in. And yet, the mere fact that we hide things from ourselves doesn't make any of these things disappear or become less harmful.

The second level is only slightly less obvious: by and large, we do not include in the price of commercial goods the costs of dealing with the byproducts that these goods generate after being consumed or discarded. For instance, in an ideal world, the potentially large cost of recycling and properly disposing—according to our best understanding of natural laws—of the remaining waste associated with every single product would be built right into the product's price. But it often isn't, since doing so would significantly discourage consumption. Who pays for the difference? Our environment, of course. This layer of hidden costs is absorbed by our atmosphere, oceans, forests, wildlife, etc.

All this has been extensively documented before; I

am not saying anything new here, just recapitulating. But there are even deeper, more subtle levels of hidden costs that hardly anyone talks about. These are the ones I want to focus on now.

Consider, for instance, the way we have turned *sentient life* into a seemingly inanimate *product*. The meat section of an average supermarket nowadays displays meat in the form of clean, bloodless, standard-shaped cuts lying on a dish and wrapped in plastic foil. The result looks nothing like a living being; it could as well have come straight from an automated manufacturing line. The steaks and chicken filets we buy look nothing like a cow or a chicken. And so the true cost of what we consume—namely, the *life of a sentient, fairly intelligent animal*—is hidden from us. Who pays for the difference? The animal that lost its life so as to allow us to eat its meat, of course.

Make no mistake, if you knew that the steak you are about to tuck into came from your own pet dog or cat, you would want things to change; the *true* cost you are paying for that steak would suddenly become glaringly obvious to you, and you would consider it totally unacceptable. For you know from personal experience that your dog or cat is not just a statistic, a number, but a sentient living being instead, fairly intelligent and with a personality of its own; a living being very dear to you.

Are things any different—that is, are the costs any less severe—when it so happens that the animal in question isn't one you are personally acquainted with? Would the life of your cat or dog be any less valuable if they happened not to be *your* cat or dog? Does your lack of acquaintance with an animal render this animal's life any less valuable than it would be if the exact same animal happened to be dear to you? Every cow, pig and chicken out there is, in potentiality, a very dear pet to someone; a deeply loved family member. And yet we kill them to the tune of millions a day. That's the true cost.

There is an even more pernicious strategy for hiding the costs associated with consuming sentient life. It is so widespread, so common, that we unthinkingly take it for granted. It is this: instead of dealing in terms of how many *lives* we consume, we deal in terms of measurement units, such as kilos or pounds. "Americans consumed X pounds of meat per capita last year," we hear on TV. It sounds so impersonal, so objective, so... normal. We consumed X pounds of meat... alright, so what? Well, how about this: "Americans *killed* and consumed X *sentient living beings* per capita last year"?

But even this doesn't really capture the *true* costs. For each and every one of those "X" sentient beings had a unique personality, a unique history, a unique inner life. To say that "Koreans eat dogs" doesn't make the cost of eating dogs clear enough. What would do the trick would be to say, "Koreans ate *Max*," *your dog*; for Max isn't an anonymous, abstract dog, but one *you know*. Max is a very real, very concrete, very alive entity. Only by knowing the *actual and complete truth* about Max can you truly understand the cost of eating Max. We only know the cost of consuming something when we are *personally acquainted* with that which is being consumed; when we know firsthand what is being *lost to the world* in order to enable our consumption. Without this, the true costs remain hidden.

Pigs and cows are sentient animals comparable to cats and dogs in almost every salient way. They are intelligent, have unique personalities, have moods, can be happy and playful or sad and depressed, etc. In the Netherlands, when cows are let out of their stables at the beginning of spring, they run around and play in an obvious display of joy. Pigs make for great pets, if only one has the space to keep them. The same applies to many other animals, including fowl. Ravens, for instance, can solve complex problems and are probably more intelligent than any cat or dog.

Instead of talking about our meat consumption in terms of pounds or kilos, or even in terms of the number of lives it takes, it would be helpful if we talked about *Sarah the cow*, *Robin the pig*, *Lily the chicken*. Each one of them—each a unique, sentient creature—would be as dear to you as your pet cat or dog, *if only you knew them personally*, the way you know your cat or dog. Their individual sacrifice is the *true* cost of our patterns of consumption: very real, unique lives lost to the world.

This reminds me of a story my dear friend Dr. Jane Goodall once told me. During her doctoral research, she used *names* to identify each individual in the group of chimpanzees she was studying. When the time came to write her thesis, she continued to identify them by their names, instead of numbers. This, it seems, got her in trouble with her supervisors, who felt it made her relationship with the subjects of her study too personal. Using numbers to identify individual chimps was—they reasoned—more objective, detached and scientific. This goes to show how much we have institutionalized our strategies for hiding the costs of our activities on this planet.

I am not saying that we should stop consuming life; except for plants—which derive their sustenance from minerals in the soil and sunlight—life nurtures and maintains itself by cross-consumption. But unlike our hunter-gatherer ancestors—who knew the costs of killing by interacting directly with the animals they hunted, seeing these animals die, experiencing firsthand the bloody spectacle of skinning and butchering them— we've hidden away the costs. *This is what is dysfunctional.* We've automated and sanitized killing, rendered it clinical and impersonal, thereby making it way too easy, way too convenient to consume life as if it came out of a manufacturing line.

Survival does have a natural cost; we can't avoid it. *But it is imperative that we be aware of this cost.* We will still kill, still consume life to maintain our own, but at least we will remember the sacrifice that other sentient beings make to allow us to live; we will perhaps even be grateful to them during each and every meal. Whether we acknowledge it or not, survival is expensive and poignant, not a sanitized matter of convenience to be taken for granted. If we were truly aware of what has been lost to the world to enable our next bite, we would perhaps consume meat in a more sober way, with considerably more moderation.

And the same applies to everything else we consume, not only meat. For every plastic bottle or straw we casually discard, Flipper the dolphin and Toothy the shark—two living, breathing, sentient beings with a unique personality and individual history of their own—choke and die a slow, agonizing death after swallowing waste plastic adrift in our oceans. How about watching your pet cat or dog dying the same death? Would that be acceptable? For every electronic device we buy, Amare and Kwame, child slaves working in subhuman conditions in African rare-earth mines—without which we couldn't make those devices—undergo unspeakable hardship. Would it be acceptable if your own child had that kind of life? For every airplane trip we make, Brutus the polar bear starves slowly to death because human-induced global warming has melted the icepacks where he used to hunt. Would it be acceptable if you had to witness Brutus shrinking to skin and bone each day?

Only by constantly reminding ourselves of the true costs of our lifestyle can we consume with *dignity* and *decency*. Anything else is, quite frankly, immoral.

Money

In the early days of human society, the concept of money didn't yet exist. People traded goods with one another based on availability and need. A farmer with a surplus of grain could exchange some of it for the surplus meat his neighbor had after slaughtering a pig. Or a craftsman could produce surplus dishes and bowls to trade for some of the eggs the old woman at the edge of town collected every day from her chicken pen. People had an *unmediated* relationship with the goods that were essential for their lives, be it grain, meat, pottery, eggs or whatever. They valued these goods in a very concrete manner: the old woman at the edge of the village knew, very poignantly, what she would *not* be able to do by parting with some of her eggs—namely, she wouldn't be able to eat those eggs—as well as what she would accomplish with the pottery she got—namely, cook and keep her food from spoiling. This sense of value was very palpable, very immediate. Essential items were traded for essential items, with nothing in between.

Trade through the direct exchange of goods and services works well at a small scale. As society grew and complexified, however, it became difficult for a person who, say, had surplus pottery and wanted eggs, to find another person who wanted pottery and had surplus eggs. And so we invented the concept of currency: an *intermediary* step in trade, which embodied in generic and abstract form the value of the items being traded. This way, if the craftsman produced a surplus of pottery but none of his customers had a surplus of eggs, the craftsman could trade his pottery for currency instead and, in turn, trade the currency for the surplus eggs of someone who wasn't interested in acquiring pottery. Money allowed trade to scale up, but also made the value of goods more abstract: when the craftsman got metal coins in exchange for his pottery, there was nothing of immediate survival utility that he could do with those coins; he couldn't eat or drink the coins, or warm himself up at night with them, or even defend himself by throwing coins at an adversary. The value of the coins was indirect, a result of a social convention, a belief, unless and until the coins were exchanged for something of concrete value, such as eggs.

Despite this, until not so long ago the value of money was at least *anchored* in real, concrete resources. We had, for instance, the gold standard: the total value of the currency in circulation in a society was equal to the value of a certain fixed quantity of gold kept in safe storage somewhere. As such, currency was a conventional representation of *real* gold and its corresponding value. We used currency instead of the actual gold because the former was more convenient and safer to circulate. Nonetheless, every commercial transaction was still directly linked to a *concrete* resource—gold, a robust metal that has many uses, not the least of which is adornment—even though this resource had become merely an intermediary.

In the 19th and early 20th century, however, we've abandoned the gold standard; all standards, for that matter. The total value of the currency in circulation is no longer linked to a concrete resource of this limited planet. Governments and central banks create and destroy currency based simply on a trade-off between economic stimulus and inflation: if there is too little currency in circulation credit becomes difficult, entrepreneurship slows down and the economy goes into recession; on the other hand, if there is too much currency in circulation prices start to increase because the value of any single unit of currency becomes diluted. This way, the value of money has finally become *entirely abstract*. It has turned into the outcome of a kind of numerical game with hardly any link to concrete resources. It has been lifted from the world of actual goods and services, and into a realm of abstraction maintained entirely by convention and belief. After all, you can't eat a banknote, or cover yourself up with it, or entertain yourself merely by looking at it. Even the value the banknote has in a future transaction—that is, a transaction that would get you something you can actually eat, warm yourself up with, or entertain yourself with—isn't linked to any concrete thing anymore. And yet we *trust* unconditionally that money has value, often by literally betting our lives on it.

All this is well known; I am saying it merely to provide context for the point I want to make now.

Because money is a necessary step between us and most things we need or want, it has become the focus of our attention not only in Western society, but now all across the globe as well, with rare exceptions. The achievement of whatever people dream of or consider meaningful in their lives has become dependent on the possession of a sufficient amount of abstract monetary units. Money has become, quite literally, the proxy for just about everything we care about. In a strong sense, it has acquired divine powers: instead of making sacrifices to the gods to get them to intervene in the realization of our dreams and to keep ourselves healthy and safe, we now seek the intermediation of money. After all, unlike the gods—with their unpredictable moods and dispositions—money *always delivers*, provided that we have enough of it.

Now, because—as discussed above—money has become a completely abstract convention with no anchoring in concrete resources, insofar as it mediates between us and our needs and dreams, our very lives have become somewhat abstract as well. Our attention is no longer directed straight to the concreteness of goods and services, but to the conventional layer that sits in between us and them. We've abstracted the reality of our lives away, at least to some degree, for the benefit of an insidious kind of make-believe. We think of money more than we think of what we (would) do with the money.

It is true that, for many of us, what we really want is that beautiful house we visualize, or that beautiful car we dream of, or that fantastic experience of traveling to a faraway land; or even something as basic as the next meal or a roof above our heads. For many of us these concrete necessities and images come first, money being just a means to an end. But for another, relatively large group of people in our society—a group that also happens to retain most of the power and influence—money has become a critical yardstick in and of itself, a kind of representation of one's self-worth. These latter people attribute most of the meaning of their lives to the accumulation of capital as an end in itself. They compare themselves to others based on how much money they have managed to hoard. For them, life has turned into a completely abstract game, a race towards an ever-larger number on a computer screen displaying one's bank balance. Like a rocket carrying astronauts to the moon, they have achieved liftoff and departed from our planet: their world is not one of concrete things, events and people—of color, form, feeling—but of pure and dysfunctional abstraction instead. This is a tragic waste of opportunity; even a waste of life, insofar as life is that series of concrete experiences we undergo on this planet between birth and death.

To be quite frank, even amongst those who consider money merely a means to an end—who dream not of money itself, but of that which money can buy—life has also become more abstract. The reason is as simple as it is inevitable: although they dream of concrete things, when these people engage in the necessary *actions* to achieve what they dream, they must focus on money. I am not blaming them for it, for it is our very social structures and conventions that enforce this on all of us. We all need at least *some* money to survive and realize our dreams, so when it comes to action it is the image of money that occupies our minds, even though the motivation behind the action may be a concrete thing.

As a result, during many of our waking hours we are not relating to the real world—the world of *immediate experience*—but to a conventional, make-believe realm of monetary units instead; we are living in an imagined future wherein we have enough money to acquire what we want, not in the palpable present. This is a great pity, for this world of ours is a world of concrete things and events, not of abstraction. We are forfeiting much of the opportunity for experience that we call life.

Those who remain aware that the numinous, nearly divine quality of money is merely the echo or reflection of what we project onto it—a projection of our own life force onto an empty receptacle that has intrinsically no value at all—live more real, richer lives. They live in the *real world*, the carrier of countless opportunities for *real experiences.* The seemingly objective value of money has no reality of its own.

There is no denying that money is a necessary commodity for our survival and helps in achieving our dreams—stating otherwise would be just naïve—but it is important to remain sharply cognizant that it is but a vehicle, whose reality consists in no more than what we attribute to it.

Resisting infinity

Diabetes runs in my family, so I try to have a healthy lifestyle and occasionally undergo wellness treatments. Once, years ago, one of these treatments had a rather unexpected side-effect: in a superbly relaxed state, the compulsive chatter in my mind suddenly ceased altogether, which opened space for a spontaneous, unfathomably rich influx of intuitive insights.

I experienced these insights with great inner clarity. Yet, I am unable to describe them accurately in words. The more I try, the more they escape me, like sand through my fingers. The best I can do is a metaphor.

Imagine that the world of sights and sounds we all share is half of a room divided in two by a curtain. Standing on this side of the curtain, I see objects I can easily describe, such as tables and chairs; I can hear people talking, smell the coffee, turn the page of a newspaper, etc.; I am in a realm where the past grows each day and the future shortens. The other side of the room, behind the curtain, is ordinarily inaccessible to me.

What happened to me during that fateful wellness treatment was this: I somehow found myself on the other side of the curtain, which I could only characterize as infinite and unitary, a realm of eternal oneness. There, nothing could be seen or sensed as such, there was no perception. When I turned around to look back, I expected to see the curtain, but I couldn't perceive it either. My contact with the ordinary world of sights and sounds was severed. Instead, I experienced an all-encompassing feeling of flow and non-resistance, such as I had never known in my life before.

All dualities faded. There was nothing and there was everything at the same time. It was timeless, non-local, endless and, most importantly, blissful. I let go of everything, including my sense of personal identity. My intellect was silenced: I was no longer burdened by my usual compulsive thinking. Instead, I allowed myself to *be thought*; to receive information from that infinite realm of oneness without intellectual interference. There, it was patently clear to me that the infinite *includes* and is *immanent* in our ordinary reality—the finite—but also *far transcends* it. The finite, in turn, is but a partial manifestation of infinity.

Subjectively, the experience seemed to last for countless eons. Objectively—whatever this may mean—it took perhaps 15 seconds. But those mere 15 seconds changed my perspective on existence, life and death forever. It was like finding out that the Earth is round, not flat; a total paradigm shift. Ordinary life represents—I now know—but an illusory confinement of our inherent natural freedom. And the only word I could possibly use to refer to what causes and maintains this confinement is... *resistance.* It is extremely difficult to explain why this particular word, so please bear with me.

In the infinite realm of oneness there is no resistance, no effort. Entering that realm is somewhat like de-clenching and relaxing every single muscle in one's body while exhaling slowly and deeply; except that it has nothing to do with literal muscles or breathing. It is a perennial letting-go. Nothing needs to be *done* to get there; on the contrary: it's all about *stopping* the subliminal, unnoticed but nonetheless intense and unceasing effort that keeps us in the finite realm of our everyday world; the effort we call 'to live.'

This became clear to me at the end of my experience, during my return to the finite: the most marked characteristic of this transition is the explicit awareness of how much *resistance* is involved. To re-enter the finite *is* to resist again. The contrast between the utterly de-clenched, free mode of being in the infinite and the highly clenched mode of the finite is remarkable.

It is this spontaneous resistance that holds all polarities of life—past/future, here/there, love/fear, male/female, etc.—apart. Without resistance, the polarities would collapse into each other because of their inherent mutual attraction, and there would remain only infinity or eternal essence. There would be no space or time, for space depends on the distinction between here and there, and time on the distinction between past and future. Resistance is what allows for extension, for the room that matter occupies, for the distinctions between this and that, for the boundaries that separate objects and living beings from one another. Without resistance, all nature would become one single, eternal being; which is, in fact, what nature *actually* is and has always been, behind the curtain of illusion.

Curiously, some fundamental aspects of our world do indeed seem to embody one or another form of resistance. For instance, matter resists changes in movement, an intrinsic property we call 'inertia' (this is why it is hard to stop a train once it is in movement, or to steer a heavy truck around a tight bend: matter *resists* attempts to change its speed or direction of movement). Organic life *resists* the so-called 'second law of thermodynamics'— according to which everything naturally tends to a state of higher *dis*order—through the energy made available by eating and breathing, which sustains the ordered structure of every living organism. Even our own psychology is often defined by the *resistance* offered by repressed emotions and subliminal opinions.

So here you have it: the secret of the very existence of our ordinary world of tables and chairs, memories and expectations, plants and animals—that is, the secret of the emergence of our everyday reality from eternal oneness—is *resistance*, in the broadest sense of the term. It takes continuous *effort* to maintain what we ordinarily perceive around ourselves, *as well as we ourselves*. Nothing is to be taken for granted; nothing is 'just so.' The polarities are *actively* kept apart. If the effort required to maintain this separation suddenly ceased, existence as we know it would collapse into a singularity. What else could this possibly suggest—if not outright *imply*—but that there is meaning and purpose behind it all?

Dancing polarities

In holding polarities apart, resistance creates continuous *tension* between opposites. By 'tension' I don't mean something negative, but simply a force, a pull. In our case, we can think of this tension as the impetus underlying the interplay between (a) male and female modes of being, (b) intellectual and intuitive modes of cognition, (c) the felt urges to give and receive, (d) the raw power of assertiveness and the enchanting power of vulnerability, and many other polarities. Our very lives rest on the dynamic tension between these opposites being maintained, for without such tension we would live in a world of static aloofness. The tension is the driving force of both people and societies; it is what makes them move, even strive; it is the impetus behind every action, individual or collective; it is the engine of both personal and social growth, *authentic* growth.

Therefore, the secret to a healthy and functional life, as well as to a healthy and functional society, lies—it seems to me—in ensuring a *dynamic harmony* between the polarities, whereby neither pole dominates, subdues or overwhelms its opposite but, instead, the tension between them is maintained. This dynamic harmony can be best visualized as a *dance* performed by each pair of opposites. The better the dance is—that is, the more refined the balance and harmony of the choreography—

the more functional is the result. The dance of the polarities isn't meant to achieve a certain goal or arrive at a particular destination, just as two people dancing a tango aren't trying to arrive at a specific place on the dance floor. The point is the *dance itself,* just as the point of sailing is to sail, not to go around buoys.

To grasp the value of life from this perspective requires a certain sense of aesthetics. As Plato suggested, beauty is truth. The most truthful, functional way of life is thus the one that entails the most beautiful dance, the most exquisite choreography. And no tango is beautiful if one of the partners is dominated or stomped into oblivion by the other, is it?

Yet, subduing one of the poles for the benefit of the other has been, consistently, throughout our history, the way we operate. Most conspicuously, we have put physical, assertive power on a pedestal, while neglecting the indispensable role of vulnerability in life, which we see as a weakness. But without the enchanting power of vulnerability life would be impossible. Think of all unborn and newborn animal life, insect larvae, fish fry, plant seedlings, etc.: how vulnerable, yet indispensable, they all are! To use assertive power is perfectly okay as long as it is dynamically balanced with the power of vulnerability, so as to maintain functional tension. Alas, even a cursory observation of our social dynamics reveals that we are far from achieving such an ideal.

There are many more examples of imbalance. Take,

for instance, how we value the intellect much above feeling and intuition, as if only the intellect could convey valid information and arrive at valid conclusions. Already since early education, this bizarre and skewed notion is inculcated in children: whatever you know through feeling or intuition is only acceptable if you can persuasively *argue* for, or *justify*, it in conceptual terms, using words and numbers. Otherwise, it's just fantasy, delusion, wishful thinking. Such devaluation of our feeling faculty amounts to a veritable amputation. It artificially and arbitrarily cuts us off from capabilities nature has endowed us with for a reason. It's like voluntarily gouging out an eye and believing we are better off for it. Because the amputation is not as immediately visible as a missing limb or eye, we don't realize the magnitude of our loss.

Moreover, the intellect expresses itself innately through *discrimination:* it is always attempting to draw a line between true and false, right and wrong, valid and invalid, appropriate and inappropriate, belonging and not belonging, etc. Choices made through intellectual mediation are thus intrinsically *exclusionary:* they exclude what we judge to be false, wrong, invalid, inappropriate or not belonging. In contrast, choices mediated by the feeling faculty—heart-based choices— tend to be inclusionary, to draw things and people together based on their unique strengths and relative value. Consequently, our tendency to value the intellect much above the feeling faculty leads to the myriad ways in which our society excludes people, communities, countries, animals and even nature at large.

One of the most recognized imbalances in our society and way of life is that between male and female modes of thinking, feeling and acting. Therefore, correcting this particular imbalance also gets most of our attention and effort. The problem is that, even in contexts or situations wherein women have managed to break through the glass ceiling and achieve positions of influence, the price they pay for doing so is often to sacrifice their very femininity by imitating the dysfunctional behavior of men. This is too high a price, for it defeats the very purpose of the effort to reduce the imbalance in the first place. Indeed, the detrimental imbalance here is not merely a question of gender, but of *modes of being and acting.*

If our society embodied a proper dynamic balance between male and female modes of being—regardless of gender—we would arguably be seeing less dysfunctional competition, less wars, less loneliness, more understanding, more sharing and compassion. There is much to be gained by working towards a dynamic balance.

But in order to do so, we must be prepared to revise our values. Balance can only be achieved if each pole is valued on its own terms, *not in terms of the qualities of its opposite.* This is a subtle but crucial point. For instance, male business leaders who sincerely want to contribute to a better balance between male and female principles at work may still value the intellect and assertive power above intuition and vulnerability; and so, they will support and promote women who think and act like men. At the end, no balance is achieved.

Proper dynamic balance requires a kind of cognitive leap that enables one to contemplate each pole from an Archimedean vantage point; a neutral perspective from which one can objectively assess the polarities within their total context, recognizing their respective contributions to the whole. It is extraordinarily difficult to attain such a neutral vantage point, for we are all immersed in the values we happen to embody. Yet, attaining it is essential if we are to live harmonious, functional lives. This is the key challenge at hand, and it is formidable.

Bringing it all together

By resisting the infinite oneness that is the source and ground of our being, we find ourselves living in this finite realm, whose dynamics are driven by the tension between opposites. We resist the past through guilt and regret, the future through fear, our deepest feelings through compulsive thought, the feminine and vulnerable in us through brute assertiveness and control, etc. We are always trying to get somewhere, do something, instead of just *allowing ourselves to be*; to be thought, to be felt, with less or even no resistance. We are tools, only God is a true agent. Yet we feel torn, split between polarities, for we've forgotten—since achieving some level of control over our natural instincts—how to live in dynamic harmony with conflicting forces and dispositions. We constantly wrestle with questions such as when we are going to die, why we are here in the first place, what we should do, and what the meaning of it all might be.

Clearly, we need guidance. And guidance we can have, for we are all equipped with direct channels of communication—our mental and feeling faculties—to an infinite realm of oneness, where the primordial wisdom underlying all existence holds sway. Through these channels, the infinite can 'in-form'—literally, *bring into form*—our lives, rendering them more meaningful, functional and harmonious.

Informed by the infinite, we have the opportunity to explore the myriad paths of exploration and self-development that are available to us in the finite. Despite the canned, standardized way of life that seeks to assert itself at our expense, it is still possible to live according to our own intuitive motivations and dispositions. We don't need to comply with the arbitrary social script about what a good life should entail, which we inherit from our culture. Each of us brings within ourselves a unique seed from the infinite, a unique outlook that seeks to grow and develop into the life we are meant to live. Despite all social pressures, if we dare do so we can still pursue our own path, bring into the world that which wants to be born in the world *through* us, and learn from the world what is required for our development as sparks of consciousness.

The unique path in front of each one of us can be pursued with the aid of goalposts, markers on the way that give us a sense of direction. But these 'goals' aren't to be confused with the purpose of our lives. The latter is whispered into our ears through the unencumbered feeling faculty, and often cannot be expressed in words or concepts. The everyday goals we set for ourselves are mere references. To orient our lives purely towards the achievement of these discrete goals—as opposed to giving expression to the natural dispositions whispered in our ears—is like sailing for the sake of going around buoys: one misses the point entirely.

Along the way, by expressing the full richness of our inner world, we can sow in the finite the unique seed each of us carries—provided that we stay open to the infinite by keeping our mental and feeling faculties unclogged. Equally important, we can also *facilitate* the efforts of *others* towards expressing themselves, by reminding ourselves to be understanding, to seek to grasp what others *mean* as opposed to what they manage to *say*, to avoid unnecessary judgment, to give space, and to remain open to forms of expression that may be uncomfortable to ourselves. This tolerant and empathic attitude is particularly important when we are dealing with children, for their natural, instinctive drive to express themselves may be permanently curtailed by how adults react to their behavior in early life.

As we make our way through life, we aren't alone: even though our individual path is unique, we come across many other travelers along the way. Intrinsic to these encounters is the need to both cooperate and compete, depending on circumstances. In cooperation, we and our fellow travelers can support each other as a community driven by a common orientation. In this community, each one of us plays the role of a cell in a larger organism, our activities being subliminally orchestrated by a boundless field of infinite consciousness; a field immanent in the finite, to which we are all subliminally connected.

The field of universal consciousness—if we are attuned to it through unencumbered mental and feeling faculties—coordinates even our competitive activities, rendering them functional; for little mobilizes more energy and provides more focus than constructive contest. What is important, however, is the realization that the meaning and purpose of competition is not to defeat or get one up on a fellow traveler, but to create and hold the tension required for optimal engagement with life.

Both competition and cooperation depend on effective communication, which entails the use of language. And here extra care is in order, for language has severe shortcomings when it comes to expressing our inner life to another human being. In building our entire society around concepts expressed in words, we automatically devalue all aspects of life that are not amenable to words, such as our feelings and intuitive insights. The resulting imbalance renders us practically blind to a great many things of crucial importance for our journeys. Once again, it is important that we seek to understand what is *meant*—despite the words—as opposed to what is actually said.

Ultimately, our life journey is the vehicle, the platform we—that is, our consciousnesses—have to develop or unfold ourselves, to *grow* in an organic sense, to realize our intrinsic potentials. This peculiar state of consciousness we call 'life' is an opportunity, the embodiment of a universal longing for growth. And it isn't to be taken for granted, for it is so easy to waste the opportunity if we think, feel or behave dysfunctionally.

Indeed, most of the difficulties we encounter in the journey of life have to do with subtle acts of self-sabotage. We've found countless ways to impair ourselves, and yet have little clue that this is what we are constantly doing.

For instance, by being always busy with our own self-generated, circular patterns of thought and emotional dramas, we clog the channels linking us to infinite oneness. As a result, we fail to attend to the intuitive influx of insights that is always knocking on our door; we fail to find the path we are meant to travel; fail to communicate and thereby cooperate and compete functionally with fellow travelers; fail to express ourselves adequately; fail to plant the seed we carry and, finally, fail to harvest the valuable lessons our brief stay in the finite realm offers us for the benefit of our growth.

Moreover, by focusing our energies and activities purely on solving practical problems—that is, on utilitarian things—we certainly make our lives more effective in a certain sense, but then lose from sight what we are alive *for*. There are a great many 'useless' things that are critical for our growth. Art, for instance, is what keeps us connected to our source, yet it is regarded in our society as mere decoration, or a superfluous nice-to-have. On the other hand, hoarding money is regarded as one of the most legitimate activities of life, yet it is largely an abstraction that distracts us from what is *truly* important, such as growing together by loving one another. The imbalance with which we judge the importance of the different activities we engage in is a form of self-sabotage. Unfortunately, most of the times we only realize it when we are about to die.

Living well and meaningfully isn't a given; it takes fine-tuned attention and constant loving care—that is, a good life needs to be continuously *maintained*. The intuitive voice within each of us cannot be heard unless it is nurtured and maintained through outward silence. The difficulty here is that our entire society and culture conspire to distract us away from silence, away from our inner world, away from ourselves and the true ground of our being.

Nonetheless, society and culture are nothing but the aggregate results of the thoughts, feelings and behaviors of individual human beings. There is nothing to our society but ourselves. Therefore, more than victims of our time, we are also the creators of our time. Society and culture change as we change, evolve as we evolve, develop as we develop. Amazingly enough, the key to our dreams and the solution to our fears has always been in our hands.

This little book is the result of decades of observation, learning and, perhaps most importantly, *error*. As I write these words, I am completing my 75th year. What strikes me most, in hindsight, is how much I've erred. To err is inevitable, it seems to me. Not only that, error is also *necessary*, for it humbles us, takes our focus away from our narcissistic tendencies and opens tangible space for new insights. Each error pushes us a little farther away from ego and closer to oneness, the true ground of our being. The vacuum opened by error attracts, primes or potentializes insight. And error *teaches* more effectively than anything else, for a lesson learned from the pain of error becomes imprinted in our whole being, as opposed to remaining at a merely conceptual level. Indeed, error has been the living matrix where this book was slowly incubated over the decades.

Thus, my hope is that the observations in the foregoing help you err *well*, better than I did. To err is inevitable, what is important is to catch the lesson that arises from each and every error. May this book provide you with a context, a set of reference points to help you position yourself—along with your errors—in life and world, so you know how to deal with your own experiences and insights as you make your way through this amazing journey. For however desperate or painful our situation, a critical lesson I have been taught by my own errors is this: life is worth the price.

And now, silence

Everything that was to be said has now been said. Is this thus the end of the journey represented by this little book? No, it is scarcely the beginning. For what is *expressed*—such as the foregoing words—is but half the equation. What is expressed is *given*; it looks for hands to be received; it moves *outwards*; it makes its presence and intentions *known* and *explicit*; it *broadcasts* its message so as to find those who need it; it is *active*, it *seeks*, it *unfolds*.

But there is something else; something other than what is expressed; something at least equally important. And, of course, this something cannot be... well, *expressed*. Herein lies one of the most important riddles of life.

I shall call this ineffable, inexpressible facet of life 'silence.' Silence is not noticeable in and of itself, but solely through the *absence* of something else; it is seen only when that which disrupts it ceases. It doesn't make its presence known; it doesn't move outward but inward. Silence is passive, not active; it incubates instead of unfolding; it is ground, foundation; it doesn't itself happen, but is the space wherein everything else does happen. Perhaps most poignantly, silence doesn't have an *ambassador*, for an ambassador needs to speak. When, for the first time, I came to realize this, tears welled up in my eyes; the talker in me was silenced; no words.

I cannot speak *about* silence, only *around* it, in the

hope that you pick it up with your peripheral vision. Silence is rich, infinite. Indeed, it is the philosopher's stone. Although it contains nothing, it isn't empty, for it embodies the *potential* for everything that can ever be. Silence is the matrix of existence, the soil from which everything grows. It is potential, the womb, the cave where nobody has been, the blackholes in space. It is what we are after everything we *think* we are fades away. It is the pre-existing in all existence; that which remains after everything else is gone. Silence is so close to you, so incredibly close, that you can't see it. Indeed, it *is* you; and also *beyond* you; *beyond us*.

Hence, I sign out by wishing you good fortune in the magical journey that now starts; a journey through and towards silence; a journey about which nothing can be said.

And thus now, just silence.

IFF
BOOKS

ACADEMIC AND SPECIALIST

Iff Books publishes non-fiction. It aims to work with authors and titles that augment our understanding of the human condition, society and civilisation, and the world or universe in which we live.

If you have enjoyed this book, why not tell other readers by posting a review on your preferred book site.

Recent bestsellers from Iff Books are:

Why Materialism Is Baloney

How true skeptics know there is no death and fathom answers to life, the universe, and everything

Bernardo Kastrup

A hard-nosed, logical, and skeptic non-materialist metaphysics, according to which the body is in mind, not mind in the body.

Paperback: 978-1-78279-362-5 ebook: 978-1-78279-361-8

The Fall

Steve Taylor

The Fall discusses human achievement versus the issues of war, patriarchy and social inequality.

Paperback: 978-1-78535-804-3 ebook: 978-1-78535-805-0

Brief Peeks Beyond

Critical essays on metaphysics, neuroscience, free will,

skepticism and culture

Bernardo Kastrup

An incisive, original, compelling alternative to current mainstream

cultural views and assumptions.

Paperback: 978-1-78535-018-4 ebook: 978-1-78535-019-1

Framespotting

Changing how you look at things changes how

you see them

Laurence & Alison Matthews

A punchy, upbeat guide to framespotting. Spot deceptions and

hidden assumptions; swap growth for growing up. See and be free.

Paperback: 978-1-78279-689-3 ebook: 978-1-78279-822-4

Is There an Afterlife?

David Fontana

Is there an Afterlife? If so what is it like? How do Western ideas

of the afterlife compare with Eastern? David Fontana presents

the historical and contemporary evidence for survival of physical

death.

Paperback: 978-1-90381-690-5

Nothing Matters

a book about nothing

Ronald Green

Thinking about Nothing opens the world to everything by
illuminating new angles to old problems and stimulating new
ways of thinking.

Paperback: 978-1-84694-707-0 ebook: 978-1-78099-016-3

Panpsychism

The Philosophy of the Sensuous Cosmos

Peter Ells

Are free will and mind chimeras? This book, anti-materialistic
but respecting science, answers: No! Mind is foundational to all
existence.

Paperback: 978-1-84694-505-2 ebook: 978-1-78099-018-7

Punk Science

Inside the Mind of God

Manjir Samanta-Laughton

Many have experienced unexplainable phenomena; God, psychic
abilities, extraordinary healing and angelic encounters. Can
cutting-edge science actually explain phenomena
previously thought of as 'paranormal'?

Paperback: 978-1-90504-793-2

The Vagabond Spirit of Poetry

Edward Clarke

Spend time with the wisest poets of the modern age and of the past, and let Edward Clarke remind you of the importance of poetry in our industrialized world.

Paperback: 978-1-78279-370-0 ebook: 978-1-78279-369-4

Readers of ebooks can buy or view any of these bestsellers by clicking on the live link in the title. Most titles are published in paperback and as an ebook. Paperbacks are available in traditional bookshops. Both print and ebook formats are available online. Find more titles and sign up to our readers' newsletter at

http://www.johnhuntpublishing.com/non-fiction

Follow us on Facebook at

https://www.facebook.com/JHPNonFiction

and Twitter at https://twitter.com/JHPNonFiction